AF493098

# GOLDEN BRUISES

## A MEMOIR OF SURVIVING CHILDHOOD

PAUL GILLISPIE

Golden Bruises
Copyright © 2025 by Paul Gillispie
All rights reserved.
No part of this book may be reproduced, stored in a retrieval system, or
transmitted in any form or by any means—electronic, mechanical, photocopying,
recording, or otherwise—without prior written permission of the publisher,
except for brief quotations used in reviews or scholarly works. Any unauthorized
use of this publication to train generative artificial intelligence (AI) technologies is
expressly prohibited. Infinite Pages Press also exercises their rights under Article 4
(3) of the Digital Single Market Directive 2019/790 and expressly reserves this
publication from the text and data mining exception.
This is a work of memoir. Names, identifying details, and certain events have been
changed to protect the privacy of individuals. Any resemblance to actual persons,
living or dead, beyond matters of public record, is coincidental.
First edition, 2025
Published by
Infinite Pages Press
Library of Congress Control Number 2026903151
ISBN: 979-8-9933990-0-3
Printed in the United States of America

*For showing me what real love doesn't do.*
*To my everything. My husband. My Bubba.*

&

*To Paulie and all the other little boys from the Angelo's.*

# GOLDEN BRUISES

"Today *is* the future. *Right?*"
  -Paul Allen Whitmore II 2005

"Today is the future you fought so hard to see."
  -Paul Allen Gillispie 2025

# FOREWORD

Born in the 1970s, I grew up in Pomona, CA, during the late 1980s. The winds of change were shifting into unfamiliar territory, which diminished the comforting notions of love, peace, and soul. Even the sturdy Jacaranda trees seemed to be bracing themselves for what was coming.

The new Crack epidemic had a way of transforming entire neighborhoods overnight, turning addresses into dope houses in an instant.

Lights and sirens filled the air like gospel, with distant gunfire popping off, and the ghetto bird hovered overhead like an alien demon.

Amid that noise, I was there: an outgoing, funny little kid trying to understand gangs, grown-ups, and the difference between myself and the other boys—all at the same time.

I learned that belonging to a church still left me unseen. Religion and the Holy Ghost were supposed to move through us like fire, but mostly what I felt was an awareness that I was different—that the world inside my mind didn't match the one they kept preaching about.

So I sang the songs, bowed my head, lifted my hands... and kept my questions to myself: Questions about why God spoke so loudly about some sins and so silently about others. Questions about why the people meant to protect me were often the ones who hurt me the most. Questions about why those who once embraced me in love now came after me, gnashing their teeth.

But here's the thing: even in the middle of all the chaos, there was light. A stubborn sliver of light in me. The kind that sneaks under the cracks of locked doors—one that I refused to let anyone extinguish.

I didn't know it then, but the story had already begun—the story of my struggle for survival, about addiction and memory, the arduous journey I'd make toward individuation, and about the heavy ways a child learns to carry more than he should ever have to.

Memories are the magical stuff shimmering around the good and bad times that form us all. We use them to determine how we react to the world around us. My world is flooded with memories —from the dearest to the most terrifying. Some I've shared openly; others I've held inside—until now.

Growing up in the 1980s was not for the faint of heart, and let's face it, many of us didn't make it because of that reality. We learned independence and responsibility early on, along with a high level of accountability.

Some of us felt the lasting sting of child abuse, the shame of sexual abuse, and watched gangs and this new thing called crack cocaine eviscerate entire communities—all while learning how to program the VCR and finish a Rubik's Cube without moving the stickers.

Above all else, we learned to keep our mouths shut—not because we were inarticulate or detached from our feelings, but because the generation before us convinced us that silence was the best way.

Instead of dealing with our pain, we pretended not to have any.

We put our finger over the sun and told ourselves it wasn't there, ignoring all the weight the world placed on our shoulders.

So we packed our own lunches, checked our own homework, and cleaned our parents' houses while they went to work.

We kept the belt marks and bruises hidden, along with the house keys we wore around our necks.

Those keys now serve as an ironic symbol—unlocking the stories behind the memories I tried to outrun for so long.

This is the story of my golden bruises—starting from where they began.

# 2385 CHANSLOR STREET

*A*s the California sun beamed from its familiar place above me, I sat alone on the gravel steps just outside our unit, thumbing through my homework papers while wrapped in the gentleness of a quiet breeze.

All the apartment complexes in our little neighborhood looked more or less the same—four units each, with the front apartment boasting the extra perk of a fireplace, three bedrooms, and two bathrooms.

The others, like ours, made do with two bedrooms and one bath. We lived downstairs in the second unit, right behind my grandparents, in a small corner of the world marked by a gated patch of yard that felt private enough to call our own.

On one side sat a concrete slab with a small, pitiful square of dirt beside it. As a child, I believed with all my heart that grass should grow there—that somehow, if I wished hard enough, it would.

Every week, I asked why it hadn't, and every week I was told the same thing: *the big caterpillar tree is blocking out the sunlight, Paulie.*

It wasn't much, but it was ours—a place to play, to daydream, and for a while at least, to feel safe in between moments of chaos.

Neatly wedged between the pages of an *Encyclopedia Britannica* were my workbook papers and a freshly sharpened pencil topped with a brand-new pink eraser. I was one of those kids who liked everything just so.

Each afternoon, I'd open the encyclopedia and lay my home-work packet on top, using the smooth inner pages as a desk so the textured cover wouldn't make my handwriting crooked or sloppy —like the other boys in my class who didn't seem to care about such things.

Stacked neatly on the step above me were three paperback books that followed me everywhere: *Charlotte's Web*, *Stuart Little*, and *The Trumpet of the Swan*. Aunt Gina, my favorite aunt, sent them all the way from Virginia, where my uncle was stationed with the U.S. Navy. Keeping those books close was like having her by my side.

Sheltered in the shade of the surrounding apartment buildings, I escaped into their worlds—imagining myself on the farm where Fern and Wilbur became friends, or on Stuart's brave search for his beloved Margalo. It was an escape from the precarious place I knew as home.

Everyone called our neighborhood The Angelo's, named for Angela Street, which marked its entrance. The area was a lively patchwork of people—Black, Mexican, Vietnamese, and a few White families who hadn't joined the exodus to San Bernardino and Orange Counties in the late 1960s.

The neighborhood was sliced in half by an alley, with Angela Street along one side and Chanslor Street along the other. There were two entrances—north and south—which, in time, the police learned they could block off with patrol cars whenever an APB went out for any Black male in the area.

Comfortably perched on the step, surrounded by my schoolwork, I heard a familiar voice.

Yahzmin was heading up the walkway, framed by lush green ivy and the orange-fruited branches of a loquat tree, she was deep in conversation with herself again—loud enough for everyone within a hundred-foot radius to hear.

Unintentionally, this pitiable, mentally broken woman would climb her way into the peace-filled moments of others, belting out eerie phrases with no ability to filter herself.

Those living in the apartments across the ivy opened their dining room windows one by one to look out, but once they saw it was only her, they went back to their business like nothing was wrong.

She couldn't help it anyway. *Touched in the head* was what they called it back then, with little concern for the root of the problem, so long as she wasn't causing any real shit to go down in the neighborhood.

Crazy, everyone could deal with. It was the heavier novelties— gang wars, crack cocaine, and drive-bys—that were ripping apart the fabric of our lives.

Vexed as usual by some haunting grip from her past, Yahzmin erupted, "Sit yo mutha fuckin ass back down and shut the fuck up. I'll knock yo retarded ass clean the fuck out!"

Calmly—but with justifiable concern—I watched as she walked closer on that breezy California afternoon. More worried about someone bothering her than her bothering anyone else, I waved her over.

Usually she wore a tank top and short shorts. The long lines of her muscle-toned arms flashed with strength, and so did her legs as she walked—ominously, endlessly—up and down that neighborhood every single day. Most days, she had on the same brown, worn-in leather tie-up sandals.

And she was always talking. Talking and talking and talking.

Not to anyone standing there, but to the invisible crowds gathered in the dark corners of her mind.

Trying to bring her back gently, I called her name with a softened lilt, careful and questioning.

"Yahzmin...?"

"The fuck did I say!"

She snapped at the air in front of her, face iced over with a look meant to command obedience. I knew it wasn't for me.

So I tried again, firmer this time.

"Yahzmin, it's me. It's Little Paul. Paulie."

The scowl above her brow loosened, melted, turned warm—almost glowing—like a TV mother greeting her child home from school. When she spoke again, her voice shifted into something melodic, drawn out, and sweet-like.

"Hey baaaaby... how you doin', beautiful one?"

A woman from an upstairs window across the way leaned out.

"You alright down there, Lil' Paul?"

She knew me, but I didn't know her name.

Before I could answer, Yahzmin whipped her head around.

"Girl, who you talkin' to!"

She scanned the buildings until she spotted the woman. Their eyes locked. Yahzmin's face twisted with the insult of being interrupted.

"I know you ain't talkin' to us. Girl, we busy ova' here. Mind yo' business!"

They held a silent standoff, two women equally offended.

Then Yahzmin fired at her again.

"I see you lookin' at me. Go on, leave us alone, girl!"

She turned back toward me, eyes rolling, a satisfied smirk tugging at her mouth.

"She ain't talkin' to us," she said loudly enough for it to carry up to the window.

Then, just to make sure the woman heard her, she belted out:

"She look like her coochie stank anyway!"

"Yahzmin!"

I wanted the concrete to swallow me whole. My eyes had to be wide as saucers, my mouth hanging open in shock at the sheer audacity of it.

Hand clamped over my mouth to keep from laughing, I whispered as sternly as any child dares to speak to an adult.

"Don't say that!"

The woman upstairs sucked her teeth loud and sharp, then slammed her window shut, smacking the curtains back into place.

"Yahzmin, that wasn't nice," I said, laughter straining through, covering my smile.

"Well, neither was she."

And that was that.

Yahzmin had never hurt a single hair on my head—or anyone else's, for that matter. Shame on ol' whoever she was for her insinuation. Everybody in that neighborhood knew who Yahzmin was. If that lady knew my name, she knew Yahzmin's too.

Yahzmin was Unc' Bone's daughter.

To someone passing through—someone who didn't know any better—Unc' Bone looked like a harmless old man in a wheelchair. Social Security check. Apartment number three on Angela Street. Cross the alley, cut through the courtyard, and there you were. From the outside, you might notice the men helping him up and down the stairs in his chair, taking him out for air when he "fancied the sun."

That's what you would think if you didn't know.

But I knew.

Everybody who lived there knew.

Unc' Bone's apartment was a crack house. One of the first.

The men carrying him up and down those stairs weren't saints —they were freeloaders looking to snort cocaine, dip joints in Sherm, cook up crack, sell it, smoke it, disappear inside it. How did I know? Easy. My daddy was occasionally one of them. I grew up in the middle of it, thick as smoke, so I could explain it then without blinking, just like I can now.

Even though Yahzmin never came right out and said it, I understood what was happening to her.

I already knew enough about prostitution, pimps, and sex to put together what she left unsaid. Instead of telling it plain, she drifted into code—dialogue between her and some man who must have taken pieces of her.

Her voice would drop low and eerie when she played his part. Then it would lift into something small and trembling when it was hers. The words were filthy. Explicit. Moans tangled with pleading. Snatches of scenes where she begged for scraps of dignity.

It broke my heart.

And in that strange knot of sorrow and shame, I felt embarrassed—for her, for myself, for all of it.

Trapped in a grown woman's body, mind retreating to survive, she endured by shrinking back into something childlike. What a cold thing it is when the defenseless are held captive under the fleeting whims of sick men.

My heart was soft for her. Even then, I understood. That gives me comfort now—to think maybe she knew I knew.

"Aww, you did that wrong, baby. Look here. Let Yahzmin show you."

And she always did.

"Yahzmin gon' help you learn this school. Mmm hmm. Watch."

When we finished whatever lesson she'd decided to teach me, she'd say, "Say hi to yo mamma DeAna for me."

I'd promise I would, never correcting how she said my mother's name.

And just like that, the fog would drift back into her eyes.

Quick as white clouds turning gray.

She'd spring up from the steps, cut past the laundry room into the alley, talking and talking, popping her fingers hard, singing pieces of *Papa Was a Rollin' Stone* or whatever song was still alive somewhere inside her.

And she would walk.

And walk.

And walk.

Later that day, Dawn Marie, an abnormally large girl, and her sister Vanessa pulled me into the laundry room to play hide-and-seek.

The machines lined the walls like giant white animals, humming and shaking, swallowing quarters and kids secrets.

"You gotta hide in here," Dawn Marie whispered, shoving me behind a machine.

Chauncey banged on the door. "I know y'all in there!"

Vanessa rolled her eyes. "Just be quiet and he'll go away." None of us really liked Chauncey.

From behind the machine, they started whispering—about Yahzmin. About what men did to her. About awful things that happened. Grown-up things that I didn't even want to know. The urban legend among all the fast-ass kids in the neighborhood was that her brother and her father Unc' Bone made her have sex with them all her life, and that's why she went crazy. Yeah, amongst the kids, I said. Can you imagine how grown our bad little asses had to have been for one of us to come up with that?

"That's not true," I said finally. "Shut up! Don't say that about Yahzmin."

They laughed—not cruelly, just knowingly.

"Why, is she your best friend?" Dawn Marie teased me.

"She *is* my friend, you Jolly Green big fore headed Giant!"

I just didn't want it to be true.

People who never grew up in the hood might say we were too

young to know about these things anyway—but that was life as we knew it.

Too young to know, and too young *not* to know. Survival required awareness. If you wanted to keep yourself and the people around you safe, you learned early to stay clear of the drunken men prowling in their cars, and the dudes in the alleys freebasing themselves into oblivion.

We learned to sort lies from truth with laser beam precision. There could be no in-between to wander into, no space for confusion or innocence, or you'd wind up as a Dawn Marie and Vanessa story—retold by smart-ass kids, half-laughing, half-scared, whispering in the corner of a pissed-in, apartment-complex laundry room with a broken door handle dangling from it.

## 8 ... MY LUCKY NUMBER

My very first memory is good in its permanence—
not good in the sweet, storybook way. It's carved
into me like initials in wet cement, and it best illustrates the way
we lived at the beginning of my life.

I must have been about three years old. I can see myself
reflected in the mercury-glass mirrors glued to the corkboard
wall, wearing my red fleece onesie zipped from my left ankle to
my neck—me standing beside my very pregnant mother while she
and my father scream at each other.

Their voices cracked and sizzled in the air, bouncing off the
mirrors before crashing into my ears. I looked up through their
flailing arms—hands gripping, shoving, grabbing—and then I
tumbled sideways to the floor. That's when something small and
hot curled inside me. I didn't quite have a word for fear yet.

When they began kicking at each other like kids on a playground, I ran toward the kitchen to avoid being hit, but before I
could get there, my mother fell—flat on her behind, legs spread,
still yelling. As I rushed toward her, my father's foot caught me on
the side of my face by accident.

Flash! Tiny specks of light swirled into darkness. The whole room hummed.

Bam. Bam. Bam.

My grandfather came pounding on the front door, louder than the police, demanding to be let in. When my mother opened it, he pointed a rifle straight between my father's eyes.

Instinctively, I stood between them, one hand gripping each of their legs. Somewhere in my three-year-old mind, Bugs Bunny and Elmer Fudd were at it again. Through my busted lip, I managed, "Pop-Pop, please don't shoot my daddy."

My grandfather's rage must have been near its boiling point, but his love for me outweighed his hatred for my father. He and my grandmother took me back to their front apartment that night, shielding me from the chaos as I drifted to sleep between them.

That night became the first frame of a film I've spent a lifetime learning how to stop replaying.

Don't get the wrong idea. All that fighting wasn't a matter of my mother being abused. Please don't let even a speck of that thought enter your mind. Dianna was usually the one who started the fights in our family.

My dad couldn't live his own life for fifteen minutes without her interrogating him.

"Where were you?"

"Who is that?"

"Don't do this."

"Don't do that."

Despite her ability to aggressively handle herself, I—like most boys—was groomed to protect my mother from everything and everyone, including my father.

I was taught that women were weak and needed looking after for their own good. So I spent most of our outdoor time together grimacing at the grown-ass men hanging outside the liquor store, whistling and *oooh-babying* as we walked by.

At school, *yo mamma so stupid* or *yo mamma so fat* jokes got many a little nappy-headed kid punched square in the face. To save her ass, I even mastered the art of outwitting teachers when they asked those tricky questions about how I got my bruises, or where the pink, partial handprints on my face came from.

Even though I kept all her punches and slaps a secret. Despite my undying loyalty—despite the bald-faced lies I told to protect her from being exposed as a child abuser—she still found it easy, almost daily, to take her self-inflicted frustrations out on me.

Young Dianna's explanation for everything wrong in her life followed a short, narrow path that led straight to my father. She cultivated a seed of hatred toward him early on, and through her connection with me, I learned to blame him for everything we lacked.

"You know it's your dad's fault we only have three towels to dry off with?"

"If he had a better job."

"If he was home at night."

"If he didn't do drugs..."

Maybe those things were true. Maybe they weren't. Either way, none of it was my business. Whose fault their grown-up shit was should never have been a topic of conversation for a child.

She wanted me to despise him the way she did. That way, she could be innocent. Not the favorite—because no one who beats their child almost every day gets to be the favorite—but the victim. If I believed her, she won.

My mother once told me she had always wanted to be a nun. No one normal says that shit. No offense to any nuns tripping over their habits to read this book. Maybe she just wanted to be better—better than him, better than her parents, better than her siblings, or better than the blonde lady named Judy my dad fucked in the back seat of that beige Monte Carlo in the carport that one time.

Her behavior toward my father grew so extreme that she began sharing her violent ideas with me about how to *get rid* of him.

Yes, that kind of *get rid of him.*

The once aspiring nun told her six-year-old son that she wanted to kill his father.

One night, while keeping my mother company as my dad ran the streets—probably drinking or snorting whatever crossed his nostrils—we sat against the headboard watching television. She had moved our thirteen-inch black-and-white TV onto a nightstand at the foot of the bed. *MASH** came on, and the theme song began to play.

In the dark, the glare from the screen cast shadows across her young, beautiful face. Her hair was neatly set in sponge rollers for the next day. Looking at me matter-of-factly, she placed one hand on my forearm and said calmly, "The next time Daddy falls asleep drunk, you hold his nose. When he stops breathing, we'll put him in the bathtub and pour acid on him."

I paused. I figured I'd better agree. What would happen to me if I didn't?

"Okay," I said, as convincingly as I could.

Then came the details. "We'll watch his body melt down the drain until he disappears."

"Won't that melt the tub too, Mommy?" I asked.

"No," she said, with a hint of laughter, like she'd done this before. "It might stain it, but we can paint over it."

"Oh," I said.

I didn't want to tip her off to my complete shock. My mind swirled. *Do I agree? Do I pretend to?* Yes, fool. I had to go along with it to keep from being dispensable too.

So I agreed.

I was agreeable in every way about the absolute vanquishment of my father because I wanted my mother to like me. I needed her to. She was home more than he was, and I wanted her to stop hitting me when she needed to let off steam.

I was tired. Too tired for someone so young.

Tired of being dragged by my hair for answering too slowly. Tired of my skull throbbing in the mornings while she picked my hair before school. Tired of flinching in silence, only to get popped again.

Pop. Pop. Pop. Pop. Pop. Pop. Pop. Pop.

Her favorite number must have been eight. She always hit me eight times in a row. Cleverly, she struck the top and sides of my head, hiding the bruises from view. Not that anyone was particularly incensed. It was the early 1980s.

It felt like she took gratification in watching me fold in on myself, cowering to the floor, feeding her the temporary power she lacked elsewhere. I bent down, down, down, until my face pressed into the green shag carpet—on my knees, hands clasped over the back of my neck, earthquake-drill position, just like they taught us in school.

There we were, growing up together. Me—the reason she lost her freedom—and the spitting image of the man she made me with. That couldn't have helped.

She had been abused, too. Her rage carried the logic of jealousy: *If I couldn't be happy, neither can you.*

My mother lacked the coping skills to control herself. To her credit, she always felt guilty afterward. She'd come back gentler, wrap an arm around my cautious shoulders, and settle the scrap the way bigger kids did after pushing you down too hard—helping you up, brushing off the dust, so you could keep playing.

That was her version of love.

# BOY OH BOY OH BOY!

Like most abusers carrying their own untreated PTSD, little things set her off. My mother's rage paced restlessly across the floor of her mind, bubbling just beneath the surface. She was my very own earthquake, and like any natural disaster, there was no predicting exactly when she would erupt.

In those moments, I learned to display submission. My survival depended on my acting ability, so I developed a knack for pretending early on.

Maybe, if I squeezed out sympathy at just the right moment, she would stop—so long as I endured the humiliating pain of those thunderous, repetitive, and horrifyingly inevitable eight whacks across my head. Of course, I counted them every time. I counted like you sing along to a song you hate, hoping it will end sooner.

Submission seemed to be the answer. Submission was what she wanted, so I rationalized my way through it each time, hoping the number of blows would someday lessen—maybe down to seven, then six.

Bracing my face and head became my norm. I flinched constantly—ducked and covered, begged while yawping, "Mommy, please, please, please, Mommy, I'm sorry, I'm sorry, I'm sorry, I'm sorry, please!"

Nothing.

If I cried, she piled on with a Gestapo-esque mantra she'd learned from her own father, my Pop-Pop. Coldly, through clenched teeth, she'd hiss, "Shut up! Crying is just feeling sorry for yourself, stupid!"

No shit, Sherlock. I'm feeling pretty sorry for myself because you're beating the fucking living daylights out of my tiny little boy brain, lady.

"BOY! What did I say? BOY! Hurry up! BOY, don't look at me like that! BOY! Don't make me tell you again!"

There were countless variations of this *Boy* barrage—interrogations, commands, threats.

Boy. Boy. Boy.

Always unprovoked. Always without merit. I was a child, for fuck's sake. And I was good—mannered, thoughtful, considerate. The little boy I was deserved kindness.

Instead, there was finger-pointing and long, high-volume lectures about how I was supposed to jump the second she told me to do something. I wasn't allowed to ask questions.

Blinking was forbidden—it meant, according to her logic, that I secretly wanted to roll my eyes at her.

Let that sink in.

I was threatened with death for saying the word *no*. Oh hell no. Those two little letters could get me knocked clear into next week.

One day, while I was playing quietly in my room, I had a brave thought. I decided to do something my mother couldn't control—something rebellious, done in secret.

I wrote my name in cursive on the wall behind the dresser with a burgundy crayon.

How I came up with that idea is still beyond me. Maybe I wanted to be bad for once—then hide it so I could return to it later, after the next punishment for nothing at all.

Maybe if I wrote it pretty enough, she'd see it someday and say, *Oh, Paulie, what beautiful handwriting you have.*

Yeah. Right. Idiot.

Even if she never saw it, I could keep it for myself—a small triumph only I knew about.

I closed the bedroom door until it was almost shut, then quietly dragged the back corner of the dresser across the green shag carpet as it *sssshhhhh'd* along the floor. Dion glanced over, then went back to playing with He-Man—some action figure I had no interest in.

The box of crayons and my sharpener sat on top of the dresser. When I opened the box, the burgundy crayon stood out. I twisted it inside my Snoopy Doghouse sharpener until the tip came out needle-sharp.

Now I had to choose the kind of *P* I wanted. I knew immediately—the one from the Paramount Pictures logo at the beginning of movies. My favorite.

I brought the crayon to the gleaming white wall, holding my breath. I tested my nerve with a gentle touch, then began. The stem first, dragging the rich burgundy downward, curling into a left-facing loop. A quick swoop finished the bubble. Then the A, the U, the L—fast and fancy.

It was beautiful.

Barely an inch tall, but it was mine. I had done something without permission. For the first time, I felt grown.

I crowed silently, *I don't have to ask. I just do.*

Whoosh.

The door flew open, slamming the knob into the wall.

"BOY! What are you doing?"

All my blood turned to ice. Would it be pretty enough to save me? The odds were not in my favor.

"Boy, I know you didn't just write on that got-damn wall!"

One across my face, then the rest—eight sharp smacks to the top and sides of my head.

Pop. Pop. Pop. Pop. Pop. Pop. Pop. Pop.

A few seconds in, something happened. It came out on its own.

"No!"

I froze. *What have you done?* Dion jumped off the bed and ran. The look in my mother's eyes was pure comic-book villain—*The Slapper* unleashed.

"Don't you EVER say no to me, boy!"

The belt came next. It lasted so long that the tears dried up.

"Please, Mommy. Please."

I didn't say *stop*. Stop was the same as *no*.

"I'll slap the teeth right outta your mouth."

"Keep crying, and I'll give you something to cry about."

"Did you hear what I said?"

"Yes. Yes. Yes."

I said it over and over between belt licks until my voice was gone. I tried to cover my butt, but my hands became targets. She threatened to break them off. I believed her.

I hid my fists against my chest and waited until I couldn't breathe.

Then it stopped.

"Stay in this room until I say you can come out."

The door closed.

Eyes shut, I whispered, "Okay, Mommy."

Because of the shared walls, my grandmother heard every-thing. When it was over, she was right there—on the other side of the wall, in the room where Dianna had grown up.

After a whoppin', I'd knock gently beside my dresser. She never intervened—but she handled the cleanup.

She whispered kindness through the drywall as I cupped my ear to listen, then whispered back that I loved her.

She was the good witch of my childhood story.

"Don't worry, Buttons," she'd say. "I'll bring you some Junior Mints."

She always did. She told me I didn't have to share unless I wanted to. That love—*that* was what I hoped to get from my mother.

Dianna was broken. I wouldn't understand that for many years. I wouldn't understand why until much later.

When my grandparents moved away, the safety net disappeared. Crack had arrived in The Angelo's, and life was filled with violence and uncertainty.

We moved into the front apartment.

Finality.

The room my mother once shared with my aunt became mine and Dion's. My sister took what used to be my uncle's room. The house rearranged itself into a parallel universe I didn't want to face.

So I wished to be one of the dull kids—the ones who didn't notice anything unless you physically pointed their eyes at it. The kids who couldn't form creative thoughts, couldn't write cursive, couldn't see.

How lucky it must be to live freely, without knowing. To be one of the dimwitted ones living every single day without any real grasp on reality, dismally unaffected by the world around them.

Somebody please sign me up!

# PICK A NUMBER

*J*ust when things got bad at home, they found a clever way to get worse for me at school, too. The merciful gift of oblivion would have been welcomed because, as they say, "When it rains, it pours."

No child, no matter how tough, how intelligent, or resilient, could have prepared themselves for what came next. Enter Miss Ruth Sullivan. A disgustingly fat, pasty fish-belly shaded, hate-filled, racist, homophobic, who is, to this day, one of the lowest life forms I have ever encountered.

It all started at the beginning of my first-grade school year, when Miss Sullivan began keeping me in class during recess for no reason at all. The bell would ring, the class would jump up to form the line, and I'd hear, "NOT YOU!" She'd snatch things like books or pencils out of my hand during class, then bark at me to go and stand in the corner, her voice slicing through the room as the other kids stared.

By the middle of the year, this grown woman had installed the next level of terror. Whenever I asked to be excused to the bathroom, she began by standing behind me, pressing her hands down on my shoulders to keep me in my seat.

"Is it number one or number two?"

Embarrassed either way, I'd say the number every time, hoping to be released, but it never mattered which number it was; she'd only tighten her grip while I squirmed in panic and shame. This sadistic monster got off on causing me, a first grader, to lose control of my bodily functions, which brought the dastardliest of smiles to her face.

I was being victimized, and I felt there was no one I could tell about it. Day after day, week after week, month after month, I didn't tell. Why? Two reasons. Number one: because boys aren't supposed to complain, right? We're supposed to take it like a man and shut up with all that crying. Right? To quit acting like a little pussy and man up. So far, that's what I had heard.

The second reason was that in my mind, we had enough crap going on at home without me making myself the center of a new problem. One that, if I tattled about, would prove me too weak to handle myself.

After one of my many forced accidents, my teacher performed as usual, making fun of me in front of the other kids, coaxing them out of fear and confusion into laughing along with her.

Then, once banishing me to the coat closet for an hour or so, she let my waste fester there in my pants. Walking by the closet, she complimented the other children, each by name. Peeking in a bit as she passed by, giggling at how clever another child's answer to her question was. The witch would stick her neck out to the side, so her ear could get a better listen for whether I had started crying or not. Once she was bored with torturing me or the smell finally caused enough of a disruption, she'd call the nurse.

"Hi, it's Ruth. Yeah, it's happened again… I'll send him right over."

With the nurse still on the phone, she'd say things sweetly to

me like, "Take the pass with you, sweetheart, and hurry back now."
Sometimes, as I left, I would hear her say things like, "Oh, I know,"
and "Poor thing."

An almost crippling form of relentless, systematic humiliation
became my norm in the first grade. What a treacherously rotten,
horrible, evil bitch to actively perform this physical humiliation,
through fear and intimidation.

Now, handcrafted into being the class's one and only pariah, I
managed to have only two friends. A little girl with a huge afro
named Jennifer, who felt sorry for me, and a little blonde boy with
a bowl haircut named Ryan, who always just wanted to hump me
and anything else he could in the bushes during lunchtime.

In her high-pitched, strident tone, teetering between shrieking
and laughter, my teacher would start her incantation:

"Just look at him! Does he look like *you*, Jennifer?"

"No." She'd say with a look of sorrow. Who could blame her?
She didn't want to be next.

"How about *you*, Tigran? Does he look like *you*?"

Tigran was an all-white boy with shaggy brown hair and coke
bottle glasses who hated me anyway.

"No!"

"He doesn't seem to look like anyone in our class, *does* he? His
skin is white, but his hair is like a Negro person, *isn't* it, class?"
"Isn't it?"

"Yes, Miss Sullivan."

The whole twenty or so little voices would sing out in unison
against me, which burned like salt being poured on an open
wound.

Some kids covered their mouths in fear while they answered.
Some wrung their hands while averting their eyes to look up at
the ceiling or the floor because they felt the shame of partici-
pating in my embarrassment.

But the ones who were taught at home not to like me, or

people like me; the ones who were destined to become exactly like her, their gaze was like a laser beam penetrating the cornea of my eyes, and so I stared right back at them hard, as directly and confidently as I knew how. I learned by watching the faces of the other tough kids from my neighborhood, so I looked right back at her fat ass, too.

Mocking and scolding me there before everyone, I let the tears swell until my eyes blurred for as long as I could hold them at bay. Refusing to flinch as she walked by, while laughing and abruptly pointing her finger at my face, mere inches away from my nose.

As an act of defiance, I stayed frozen like a marble statue the whole time. Over and over, day after day, she tried to make me burst into inconsolable fits of desperation. To break me, to force me to scream out, make a spectacle of myself, and beg to be accepted or shown mercy. I would do no such thing.

Standing me at the front of the class, the wet stains streaked down the front of my tan corduroy pants. So, I'd stand up straight as an arrow, neatly tuck my shirt in, and smooth down the tips of my collar, imagining that I was balancing a book on my head.

At lunch recess, she'd put me next to the gate, all the way at the back of the school, across the grass field, next to the houses. I sang to myself all the songs I knew from the radio until the bell rang.

It only took it to happen the first time. From then on out, I knew exactly how I would handle her. She wouldn't break me, not one bit. This bitch had no clue what I was made of, and neither did those scary, punk-ass kids who now avoided me on the playground.

They had become afraid that now, if they got too close, I'd knock their little empty heads off for joining her against me.

"And why are his lips so pink? Is he wearing *lipstick*? He's not *supposed* to be wearing lipstick, is he?

"No…"

The fever-pitched call to action was always her coup de grâce:

"Maybe he's really a girl. He always *plays* with the girls. He's disgusting! Should we put him away?"

"Well, class, should we put him away?"

"Yes, Miss Sullivan!" They'd all agree.

Standing far enough away from me not to get any of my stench on her, while pointing at the back of the classroom with her index finger and the other hand on her hip, she'd erupt with, "Go get in the coat closet!"

The debasement lasted for months, and with it came a heaviness I bore secretly and without complaint, the way I thought little boys were supposed to. I hadn't dared tell my mother about the terrorism at Philadelphia Elementary School. She wouldn't hear about it from my mouth. I had no intention of adding my problems to the serious troubles at home.

I made peace with my decision to keep my mouth shut. When I went to the nurse after soiling myself, she let me clean up in the private bathroom. I'd turn on the shower and stand there fully clothed for just a minute.

The soft, warm water streamed against the top of my head, helping me forget the harshness of life—at least for a moment.

It was something fun I'd never be allowed to do at home anyway—wearing clothes in the shower. I pretended I was in a forest under a waterfall I'd discovered, surrounded by trees and birds singing.

Reality called me back, so I'd take off my shirt and hang it on the knob, then carefully peel off my pants and underwear.

Turning them inside out, I laid them on the floor so the water could wash most of the mess away as I cleaned my body, trying desperately to make myself new again.

I scrubbed the seat of my pants and underwear dutifully with the scratchy, lemon-scented powdered soap from the wall dispenser, determined to erase every trace. After wringing them out and drying myself off, I wrapped the towel around me.

Relaxing momentarily into the heaviness of defeat. I let myself cave into what it meant to feel like less than nothing.

I wanted to draw a happy picture in my mind, to sing a song or whistle something, but the shame I felt spread like a black crayon across a white canvas, making a dark cloud over the yellow, happy-faced sun I wished I could draw in the corner.

The nurse handed me a black plastic bag for my clothes. After tying it in a knot, she said, "Go pick some things from the lost and found to put on, Dear."

I took my time along the walk home, hyping myself up to accept my fate, mentally preparing for my second unjust punishment of the day.

When I reached the front step, my mother started screaming at me about acting like I didn't have any common sense.

"This doesn't make any damn sense, boy!

"Why didn't you ask to go to the bathroom?"

"What's wrong with you?"

"You know how to hold it!"

I'd apologize with the look I thought a regretful person should give. Then I'd brace myself for the slaps or the pops on the head or the thundering whack across my butt—her open hand, her fist, or whatever she happened to be holding at the time.

After a while, though, Dianna surprised me. I think she started to blame herself for what she understood to be my incontinence.

After all, she was the only other person besides me who knew exactly how hard she hit me whenever she did. So she stopped beating me for coming home after a bathroom accident. She must have started getting suspicious that there was more to this than met the eye.

The nurse told me I suffered from a "serious nervous condition"—whatever that was. She said that after about my third visit, and she couldn't have been more right.

I wanted to say, "Girl, you only know the half of it! Let me tell you what happened at my house last night!"

# LET IT OUT

On a day like most others, I was banished again to the closet. It was getting close to going-home time, which meant the class would play a game soon.

For the first time, I hadn't been excluded right away. I thought —this was it. I had earned the right to play after all my torture. I had paid the price for all the flaws my teacher hated about me.

I smiled big and lined up next to the other boys and girls. They seemed excited for me, too.

Relieved to find my place between the two people closest to my height, I wedged in tight like a sardine, hoping to blend. Then, in a flash of remembrance, my teacher recalled her hatred for me and promptly banished me to the coat closet.

The other kids resumed their faithful duty of ignoring me so they wouldn't be subjected to her cruelty. Within the commotion, I got away with leaving the door open just a crack—just enough so I could feel like I was out there playing too—with the worthy kids.

The beautiful, faultless bunch who could laugh and play and

smile at one another freely. They touched hands and giggled, switching places as they lined up by height, paying each other compliments like "Well, you're taller than me." They fussed over each other with caring instructions: "Be still," or "Let me fix your hair."

At least, this time, the classroom door was open, so I could look outside when I got too sad.

The warm sun was shining, and the trees were full of green leaves dancing in the wind while clouds passed through the soft blueness of the cool spring sky.

I noticed a familiar figure standing about three feet from the door. Rollers in her scarf-covered hair. She was wearing some of the same clothes my mom had, too.

This couldn't be my mother. My mother never went out of the house with rollers in her hair. And in a scarf too? No way! That lady wasn't my mom... but she sure did look like her.

Besides, why would my mom be picking me up anyway? I always walked home from school by myself.

Then I thought, what if this was her? If this were my mom, and I could get her to see what was happening to me, this could all end with my mother beating the living shit out of Miss Sullivan.

I stuck the fingers of my right hand out of the crack and wiggled them slowly to signal her. If this were my mom standing there incognito, she would know my hands because we have the same hands. The same way the fingernails were shaped, the space between our index finger and thumb—yeah, she'd know it was me.

This just had to work.

It took her all of three seconds to notice. Her neck stuck out in disbelief. I wiggled my fingers faster, which made her eyes widen, her face turned a pinkish shade of red, then POW!—she bolted into the classroom toward me.

"Miss, you can't come in here. My class isn't over."

With one hand, my mother slung open that coat closet door right off the track, crashing down sideways and landing flat on the floor in front of her.

I was saved. Her face was dampened with a look of slight gratification. It also glared with the certainty that revenge was coming next.

My mother unleashed her most ferocious booming voice, carrying in it enough bass to shake the macaroni art right off the walls.

"Are you fucking crazy putting my son in this closet?"

She didn't give Miss Sullivan the chance to respond.

"You have lost your fucking mind, bitch!"

I felt safe now—the case was cracked.

Now she knew the whys about all this pissing myself and shitting my pants.

Now Miss Sullivan would pay. Oh, my God, was she gonna pay!

I had a front-row seat, and she was gonna get it now, Jack! If my mother beat her the way she beat me for mostly nothing—ooo wee!

All the other kids ran over to us. They came and stood next to my mom and me, siding with us in protest to finally be free of our warden.

The bell rang, so all the kids scrambled to grab their lunch boxes and backpacks from what used to be my prison.

Stepping on top of the fallen closet door panel, they made a beeline out the door.

Boys with bowl haircuts and girls in pilgrim dresses booked it across the grass.

My mother, despite her rage, managed to have a moment of clarity. Instead of doing what I knew she could do, she took me directly out of there and over to the front office, where we told on Miss Sullivan together, and this time it was okay to tell.

As we walked, my mother wrapped her other arm around me tightly. She was her loving self in this moment. Kind, gentle, and the scowl that she didn't notice wearing most of the time had disappeared. The guilt of being born and ruining my mother's life was all but crippling for me as a child. So any form of softness from her lifted that, at least momentarily.

Mrs. Hale, with great patience, took down every single word on a yellow legal pad.

They told me it was okay.

They told me *I* was okay.

They told me I was brave.

I felt brave, but mostly, I felt tired as I finally let myself experience the weight of this prolonged sadness.

For one of the few times I could remember, I allowed myself to feel self-pity—not only because of the humiliation, but because I had been forced to bottle it all up.

I could finally breathe out.

So I wept.

Sitting there, weary and worn down in one of those yellow plastic school chairs with metal legs, I melted into a small heap of a broken little person.

This time, no one told me I was only feeling sorry for myself. No one blamed me. No one reminded me that boys don't cry. Instead, I was allowed to weep freely, letting the grief escape into the sky as if it might leave my body forever.

With every gasp between sobs, I felt the freshness of new air— air finally free of the hurtful words and the ogling stares.

It was as if the master's jingle bells had been unclamped from around my neck, and I was no longer a slave to my teacher's cruelty nor a spectacle for the other kids.

It's always the breathing out that we, as little boys, are told not to do. We're taught to hold our breath and stay silent—through embarrassment, humiliation, and even sexual or physical abuse. Instead of being encouraged to release any of it, we're pushed to ignore all of it.

So we master the art of walking around with our faces hardened into masks. We learn to think only as far as we're allowed, within the narrow space between the metal bars others have wedged into our minds.

We're permitted to care about tenderness and beauty only to an acceptable degree. Our hearts aren't made of sweet candy but of chiseled quartzite—formed over a lifetime of dammed-up tears that simmer into molten lava, waiting to erupt from that little boy's voice buried deep inside.

What had only been about eight months felt like an eternity— at least it would to a first grader. I had been trapped in a dark sewer of humiliation and degradation that whole time. And finally, there it was: vindication.

Deep down, I always knew I was somebody. I had to be. No one tries that hard to make you feel invisible unless you already matter.

I mattered, even if I didn't look like everyone else, even if I played with girls, and especially because I had light skin and hair like a "Negro," you racist bitch. I mattered then, and I sure as hell mattered now that I had survived.

That day, I learned what the word powerful really meant. And Miss Sullivan—no matter how hard she tried—couldn't extinguish my spark.

I returned to school after a few days and was placed, along with a few other kids, in Mrs. Nelson's class. She was a kind, gentle Hawaiian woman who treated us with compassion for the last month and a half of the year.

Nobody mentioned the miserable months that came before,

and nobody looked at me *that* way anymore. That careful, side-eyed stare that kids save for the one who's been marked as different.

We learned the ukulele. We sang songs. I ran around the field at recess until I was breathless. My pants stayed dry and I never saw Miss Sullivan at Philadelphia Elementary again.

# SUN, MAGIC, PLAY

*E*ven after the summer, I remained skittish.

Though wary of what might come next, second grade brought some much-needed relief. My new teacher, Mrs. Stone, knew what had happened the year before.

She felt sorry for me and was overly kind, which sometimes made me uncomfortable. I didn't want special treatment. I just wanted to be treated like everyone else.

"I know about that awful woman," she told me. "But don't you worry. No one is going to hurt you in my class."

Shell-shocked from the previous year—combined with all the fighting at home—I developed a nervous habit of licking my lips. They stayed cracked, sometimes bleeding, so I was sent to the nurse for Vaseline or ChapStick whenever I needed it.

The nurse, the new "good" teacher, and even the principal, Mrs. Hale, kept quiet watch over me. They could tell something was wrong at home. I knew they knew. So I said nothing.

Let's be real: growing up in the ghetto is just fucked. Trying to dress it up in prettier language doesn't change the truth. It's fucked.

From my neighborhood, I learned a whole catalog of survival skills that followed me into adulthood.

Lock every door and window. Keep a weapon by the bed. Never stand too close to the front door when you're trying to figure out who's knocking. The list is almost endless.

I learned that love meant fighting—always. I learned that the same neighbors whose kids you played with while the grown-ups slapped dominoes on the table would steal from you without blinking.

They'd call the police on each other just to lie and get a little revenge.

What disgusted me most was that even though nobody had much, there was always someone ready to drag you for having less.

"Look at them bubblegum shoes!"

If you weren't wearing "real" Chuck Taylors, a pack of kids would circle someone and chant:

*Yo shoes, yo shoes,*

*yo Kmart shoes,*

*they make you scream and holla,*

*they only cost a dolla!*

There wasn't time to question why I saw the world differently from other kids in the Angelos—no buffer space for doubt or reflection. You moved how you were taught, believed what you were told, or you paid for it.

Cursed with more awareness than a child should have, I began accumulating a kind of debt. Like the others around me, I had to pay. For knowing too much. Our innocence was stripped away and traded for a heavy currency: vigilance.

I never chased the usual traps—gangs, tagging walls, selling weed, idolizing drug dealers. Those were easy to avoid as I felt no pull toward them.

Instead, there was a beautifully stubborn spark inside me that whispered other possibilities. Better ones. I didn't know what they were yet, only that they existed.

The one thing I could never do was tell anyone how my mother beat me. That was an unspoken oath, learned under her hand.

I'd been taught since birth that telling would destroy everything. I even lied to other kids, saying my mother was a teacher and my father a police officer. Yeah...

One day, Mrs. Stone asked quietly, "What's that mark on your face, Paul?"

"Oh," I said quickly.

"I was playing with my little brother—he hit me by accident."

She blinked slowly. Inhaled. I could see her reaching into that private mental place where teachers keep their unspoken conclusions about children with marks on their faces.

She was about to say something—then stopped. Maybe she remembered where she taught. Maybe she saw what I was: a seven-year-old trying desperately to stay intact.

In the silence, I reminded myself not to look like a beaten child. I smoothed my face, lifted my cheeks into something resembling a smile.

I didn't want to be beaten for telling. I didn't want to be taken from my brother and sister. I didn't want foster care. I didn't want my parents in jail. I didn't want to be a tattletale rat bastard.

Mrs. Stone took my hand gently. Her blonde perm bounced as she leaned closer, her blue-and-white plaid dress cinched neatly at the waist. "If you ever need to tell me anything," she said softly, "I'll protect you."

I thought, *Has this woman ever met my mother?* What exactly was this tiny white lady going to do?

So I did what I always did. I knew how to make the handprint disappear. I smiled, laughed, and skipped away toward the playground like everything was fine.

That's the trick. You make it look okay. You make them believe it's okay. And eventually, you almost convince yourself.

I knew they all knew—the teacher, the nurse, the principal. Their eyes said it. So I widened my smile. Sang louder. I raised my hand more. *Ooh, ooh—me!* until the sound of my own voice made me sick.

Most days, during morning recess, I slipped into the boys' bathroom and locked myself in the last stall. I'd sit quietly, hands folded in my lap. It didn't matter if I had to go. What mattered was that I *could*. Being allowed to use the toilet when I wanted felt like freedom.

Black-and-white tiles reflected in the fluorescent lights. The room echoed with distant laughter and dripping faucets. It was peaceful. A place where no one patronized me. No one tried to heal me. No one pretending softness could undo the damage.

My first-grade teacher had crushed me so thoroughly that kindness felt like bait. Compliments sounded like setups. Pity and love seem to blur together when you need both too badly.

I was a multiracial kid created in the 1970s, born to two biracial parents. Nobody looked like me—not in my neighborhood, not even in my family. Not even my own brother. I was the odd one out.

Since I'd already heard the sermon about beauty coming from within, I decided that might be my safest bet. I turned inward—toward the part of me no one could point at or mock.

The quiet never lasted. Boys would crash into the bathroom, chanting, "Everybody show your wiener!" and "See who can pee the farthest!" A stainless-steel trough ran along one wall. Older boys climbed urinals, aiming streams like it was some kind of Olympic event. Everyone left splashed with someone else's urine.

When it was over, I slipped out and searched for Jennifer—my one safe place.

With her, I began cultivating what I later called *Gay Boy Power.*

Even then, I refused to let the world crush my joy. I wanted to laugh. I wanted to be happy and gay without shame.

I already knew. I'd known since I was four or five. I didn't have the language yet, but the truth hummed under my skin, and it shone through in all the things I did.

Despite everything, goodness still poured out of me. I stayed kind. Fighting wasn't my nature—it was just a skill I learned to survive. Love remained my first instinct, my sharpest tool.

Love and creativity—that was Gay Boy Power. Not glitter or common sass. The alchemy of survival dressed in joy. Grace in the middle of madness.

Sitting in the grass with Jennifer was my safe place. Sunlight flashing through her hair as I braided it. We jumped hopscotch in socked feet and when we didn't want to be bothered with a third person, we'd tie the ropes around a pole so we could play Double Dutch. Just the two of us laughing anyway.

In those moments, I was free. I had earned that freedom.

And when we jumped—we'd sing:

*Cinderella, dressed in yella,*
*went upstairs to kiss her fella,*
*made a mistake and kissed a snake.*
*How many doctors did it take?*
*One, two, three, four, five—I'm alive!*

# GOOD SUNDAYS

eekends away from school were always a fifty–fifty chance at peaceful. Sometimes we went out to L.A., over to 53rd and Normandie, where we stayed with my Grandma Lo-Lo and my dad's side of the family. Those weekends were usually easier. It was when we stayed home, those were the times that it was more likely that a fight would break out between my parents. If we managed to make it all of Saturday though the cartoon line-up, Soul Train and a movie on the 26" black and white screen without anything poppin off that night, we'd sometimes get lucky and wake up to one of those Good Sundays — the kind where my daddy was up early, sober, and really there with us.

He'd carry all the houseplants outside to give them a good watering and a little sunshine. Then he'd give us some sunshine, too, by getting in the kitchen and cooking for his family. Pan-fried potatoes with the skin still on. Bacon or sausage. Those under-whisked, overly peppered eggs—always a little runny, but made with a lot of love. Toast with jelly, or apple butter if there was any left. We were happy as hell to eat it, because breakfast like that meant it was going to be one of those Good Sundays again.

Dianna wouldn't have had time yet to cook up one of her million reasons to get in his face and tell him how he ain't shit, ain't never been shit, and ain't ever gon' be shit, not on a Good Sunday. It wasn't every Sunday, but on the Good Sundays, he'd say, "Paulie, come over here and help me, man," acting like he didn't already know what he was doing.

"I'm coming, Daddy!" Whatever it was, I was there. I loved it when my daddy called me *man* or *son.* It made me feel like we were on the same team—that I had some value to him.

All morning long, my daddy played albums on the record player and sang. And damn, he could sing too. I mean, really sing. He'd say, "Come on, Paulie, hit that high note with me," while Earth, Wind, and Fire's *Keep Your Head to the Sky* poured through the speakers. I'd sing my head right off my shoulders for him, too.

Whenever my daddy was outside singing, people drifted into our yard to listen. They'd stand nearby with easy smiles, a gold Miller High Life or a silver-and-blue Schlitz Malt Liquor Bull in one hand—a cigarette in the other. The neighborhood men were all trying to behave themselves because it was the Lord's Day. On a Good Sunday morning, you didn't hear arguing or police sirens. Nobody was in the alley yet, filling the air with weed smoke or trying to one-up the next man about how many women he pulled last week or how many high-school games he won back in the day.

Well…not yet, anyway.

Busy mothers weren't cussing out base-heads for smoking crack in the shared laundry room yet, and if it was hot enough, all the kids were running free through someone else's sprinklers. We'd lie out on the warm sidewalk one right next to the other, side by side, like steamy little French fries from Sam-O's burger joint until the sound of *Pop Goes the Weasel* playing from

Godwyn's ice cream truck filled the air. The promise of Bomb Pops, Big Sticks, and Funyuns sent us giggling and wiping the water from our little legs—on the run to ask any grown-up in sight for a dollar.

I'll never forget how, on a Good Sunday, my daddy's voice came over all soulful and light. He sounded like a man who wanted to do better, but didn't quite know how since no one had ever taught him. No one had yet ever unlocked anything powerful enough to make him try, either. Back then, when I was still Lil' Paul, I believed I was the only one who could do it. I thought I had that magical power. If I asked him to stay home, he did, sometimes, and when I asked him not to drink, he'd nod and say, "Okay, son." That was enough for me to rush back outside and play. Whether he kept his word for five minutes or the whole day was another story, but in that moment, he was who I liked to call my real daddy—the one I trusted.

Since I was born when they were teenagers, I always felt like a living, breathing, inconvenience to my parents, so I learned early never to ask for much. I didn't want toys, or video games, or new Adidas like the other kids. I just wanted my dad, man. That meant I needed him present. Most of all, I needed him sober. That's about all I knew back then—that my sober daddy was the real one hiding somewhere underneath the macho façade, beneath the intoxicated, crumpled mess he so often became. Though I loved all of him with all my heart, that sober version of him was the daddy I liked. The one who made Good Sundays exactly that.

Now, there were good times on other days, too, with joking and tickling, the Soul Train lines, the way we'd rest our heads on Mommy's booty while watching TV on the floor. There were water balloon fights in the street and Ding-Dong-Ditch to be played, too. Hell, once, we even had real pony rides from a travelling petting zoo. And though I clutched desperately at the happy memories that filled my heart with light and laughter during those fleeting moments, it was the heaviness of the broader, more frequent reality that pulled those carefree times away from me, causing their gentleness to drift away like a leaf in the breeze — always floating just out of my reach.

Nothing was better than the Good Sundays. But after we ate a late breakfast, cleaned the kitchen, and brought the plants back inside, the volume on our block would slowly start to rise. Being good on Sunday only had to last until all the old ladies got home from church. The distant chatter grew louder and louder, as the restless adult boys who preferred to be called men came outside calling for each other, ready to hang tough.

In my neighborhood, Good Sundays never lasted too long.

That's when Daddy started his trademark wandering around the apartment. He paced the floor, stopping to lean against the arm of the sofa, the wall, or the doorway, and looking out the window into the sky, listening for something only he could hear. Before long, he'd slip into the kitchen for a cold beer. The snap of the pop top was like an alarm, sharp and unmistakable, signaling the beginning of the end to our Good Sunday.

Pretty soon, he, along with his fan club of neighborhood guys, would be in our front yard lifting weights, talking loud, and smoking weed too, but mostly drinking themselves stupid. Talking way too damn loud, according to my mother—and cussing up a storm, too. Mothafucka this, Punk Nigga that, and that chicken head this and ol' crack hoe that. Dianna's voice would cut through it all, crisp and condescending, hands on her hips from the front doorway.

"Already?" she'd say, or, "What are they doing over here Paul?"

Most of the time, my mother talked about my dad's running buddies like they weren't even standing right there in front of her —and man, was she good at it.

"Hi, De Ann." One of the guys would offer, trying to sound

polite. Before he could even finish the sentence, she'd spit back with, "My name is pronounced DIANNA! Die-Ann-Ahh!"

Whoever they were, they'd drift off one by one, offering a half-hearted farewell.

"Aiight, main, catch you on the flipside." Then Dianna, with two n's, *thank you very much*, would go step outside to make sure they had all left.

It didn't make any sense to me anyway because the same thing would happen every time. Next, he'd change into his tan Dickies with creases you could cut butter with, brown dress sandals with white socks underneath, and put on a tank top or leave his shirt off altogether, depending on the weather. I'd be thinking to myself, *Dang, Mom, he was right there!* She'd run him off, so he'd go away to drown his pain. The pent-up pain from even before he ever became my daddy. The pain he carried from when he was a Little Paul, too. Back when he was a boy without a father.

He'd grab the rest of his six-pack or the case of beer from the refrigerator, pat my afro, kiss me on the cheek and say, "Be good, son." Dianna would slam shut, whatever cabinet door she was standing in front of, then we'd lose him to the wiles of the alley for the rest of the day and most of the night where later on he could be found propped up—leaning against a yellow dumpster, a splintered garage door, or a telephone pole to relieve himself while trying his best to spit the slurred, liquor-soaked words of a mostly made-up story, all to entertain his homeboys on our side of the alley—and just like that, the Good Sunday was over.

# THE FAMILY JEWELS

Most of the men in the neighborhood had some job or another—and you know what *another* means. They weren't called baby daddies yet, and they still played games with us out in the street: freeze tag, hide-and-seek, football. But when night fell over the block, and the streetlights buzzed on, they went looking for our next-door neighbor, Red, the dope man of The Angelos.

The women stuck together inside, where the real tea was spilled. My supersonic, nosy kid ears soaked up everything. They sat hip to hip, comparing and complaining about their low-down, dirty-dog men. They sipped Tropical Punch Bartles & James and took baby hits from a joint held in a roach clip with feathers and beads dangling from it.

Girl, this, and Honey-Child, that.

"I wish that nigga would." And,

"No, he didn't!"

That particular Sunday night, the sky was clear with a moonlit glow—that California kind of cool. My mom's friends Valentina, Joyce, and Willa-Mae had just left after the girls' gathering. People lingered on their porches, letting the kids stay out a little later than usual.

Outside, the deep voices, laughter, and boombox music gradually faded into silence.

The streetlights were already on, and even though the day had started as one of those Good Sundays, my father still wasn't home. We were stuck in the teetering space where a night could go either way, and I prayed it would slide quietly into being unremarkable.

With the clock ticking, I knew my little brother and I were supposed to be in bed by nine. I walked on eggshells, whispering reminders to Dion to do the same.

When Dianna told us to brush our teeth, I grabbed Dion by the wrist and rushed him into the bathroom before she could hear him protest.

After putting our baby sister down in her crib, Dianna stayed pensive as she walked us to our room. She tucked Dion in and kissed him goodnight. Not wanting to create any extra work, I climbed under my own covers and waited for my turn. She pulled the cord on the off-white pleated drapes until they met in the middle, then gently closed the door behind her.

As usual, Dion and I popped right back up like prairie dogs. We kicked up our neat covers and scrunched our pillows so we could face each other for our nightly meeting—where all the important things got discussed.

We went back and forth on everything that mattered, like what game we'd play after school the next day.

Whether lava could burn Superman if he stood in it long enough, and if you fell into quicksand, would you drop straight through to China, or could you hold your breath and survive? And if you did make it to China, how would you get home? Or would you just have to stay there forever?

These were the things brothers talked about when they shared a room. At least, these were the things we talked about.

We whispered nonsense until nonsense did what it always did —made the days, and especially the nights, easier to get through. Nights were always the hardest.

Eventually, our words thinned into yawns. And like we did every night of our childhood, no matter what had happened that day, no matter what fear sat quietly between us, we said the same thing to each other, "See you when the sun rises," because no matter what, it always did.

We had only just drifted off when, from the far side of the apartment near the backyard, my father's voice called us awake.

He was singing.

Mellifluous and soaked in malt liquor, his voice drifted through the apartment, sounding both sweet and unsteady. It was a patio aria meant as a white flag—coy, a little off-key, and hopeful in the way only a drunk apology can be. He sang in the style of Kool & the Gang, stretching the words as if his charm alone might open the door.

He crooned, "Di-anna—I—love you. You're the one—the one for me."

"Open the door!"

No response.

"Dianna!"

"Open the got damn door, man!"

Then, softer. Almost tender.

"Mommy? It's me. Open the door."

Whenever my daddy came home fucked up, my mother usually took it as her cue to unload every insult she'd been saving, spiraling quickly into accusations of him sleeping with every woman in the neighborhood except, of course, for the ugly ones, or her best friend Valentina.

But this time was different.

The stereo had been playing softly since the women left. Then the volume dipped. A moment later, it dipped again. I figured she was turning it down so he could hear whatever she planned to say once she finally opened the door.

As the oldest, I knew her methods by then. Still, something felt off. She wasn't loud. She wasn't raging.

Maybe that little hit of weed from earlier had mellowed her ass out.

Either way, I knew what time it was.

It was time for me to switch into *be ready for anything* mode.

My brother looked over at me, and without a word, I motioned for him to pull the blanket over his head.

For Dion, just hearing the violence was enough to break him. Once those sounds started crashing through the walls, he'd freeze in place—like one of the ashen children of Pompeii, vaporized where they stood. Everything in him went still except his big brown eyes. They widened with every slam, every scream, then filled with tears, glazing over with terror.

Each bang made his body stiffen and tremble. Anything that shattered against the floor or slammed into the walls sent his hands flying to his ears, palms pressed tight. If it went on too long, he'd push his index fingers into his ears and hum, trying to block it all out.

If I could have wished him temporarily deaf in those moments, I would have. Hell, I would've wished him into another dimension entirely—then wished him back safe again. And while I was at it, I might as well have wished us some new parents.

I knew this one was going to be bad.

I sprang out of bed and crept toward the door, moving as quietly as a ninja. Dropping to my knees, I bent forward slowly so I could peer through the crack beneath it. Across the hall, Brianna's door was shut. I pressed my ear to the wood and listened.

The vibe was eerily still, like when you wake up too early, and there aren't any cars on the street yet, and the birds haven't even started chirping yet.

I knew what that silence meant.

On nights like this, when the alley went quiet and my dad hadn't come home until late, it could only mean one thing. He had linked up with the guys and bought dope from Red over at Unc-Bone's place.

Coming home wasn't about ending the party. It was about refueling. This visit wasn't for us. It was a pit stop, meant to pillage whatever money Dianna had managed to stash away so he could head back out for round two.

First, he'd ask.

Then he'd demand.

Then he'd start tearing through the place.

No matter how it went down, he had to get that money.

Luckily for all of us, Dianna was creative. She had more hiding spots than he had patience. Every time one was discovered, she came up with another.

Inside the *Home Sweet Home* pillow on the rocking chair.

Under the bathroom sink.

Wedged between the toilet paper roll and the wall.

Some honorable mentions in the category for best places to hide the rent money included:

Behind the *Footprints in the Sand* picture in the living room, tucked inside the fireplace screen, and, my personal favorite— slipped behind the decorative, hand-painted ceramic baking dishes hanging on the kitchen wall.

But the grand prize for Best Hiding Place From A Coked-Out Drug Addict goes to: the gray-and-black ceramic plaque of *Da Vinci's The Last Supper*.

It hung there in the dining room looking holy as hell, with a secret behind it. The bills were folded neatly and flat, pressed between the wall and the plaque, right behind Jesus' head.

Then there was the backup money.

He didn't know it, but that night, he was really hunting for *that*.

The just-enough money.

Enough to keep us from getting evicted.

Enough to keep the lights on.

Enough to make sure we had food and diapers until the next county check came through.

One afternoon, while she was sitting on the sofa in front of the window, she called out to me.

"Go get my purse."

"Okay."

I knew exactly where it was.

When I brought it back, she opened it and dumped everything onto the coffee table. A red wallet. A compact. Lipstick. gum, along with a couple of unpaid bills.

"You see this zipper pocket?"

"Yes."

"Open it."

I did.

"Stick your hand in there. Can you feel the hole in the liner?"

"Yes."

"Take the money out."

It was rolled tight in a blue rubber band. I wrapped my little hand around it.

She clamped her hand over mine, firm but calm, and gave me my instructions.

"If you ever hear me and Daddy start fighting really, really bad, I want you to take this money out of my purse and hide it in the front of your underwear."

"Okay, Mommy."

There was no panic in her voice. No drama. Just preparation.

Like she was teaching me how to cross the street. Or tie my shoes.

Now I was back in the present, my ear still pressed to the crack beneath the door. I could feel it—this was the moment. If I waited too long, it would be too late.

I had to get to my mother's purse before the bomb dropped.

She kept it under the bed on her side, tucked between the back frame leg and the nightstand. I stood up slowly, wrapped my hand around the brass-colored doorknob, and turned it as gently as I could.

I slipped through the narrow opening and bolted down the hall into my parents' room.

The purse was right where it always was. I unzipped the pocket, and there it was, like buried treasure. I clutched the roll tight in my fist and ran back to my room.

Pulling the front of my underwear forward, I shoved the money inside, then just stood there, breathing shallow and quiet, waiting.

But nothing happened.

No yelling. No crashing. No chaos.

Had I moved too soon?

And that's when the worst thought crept in.

Maybe she had gone ahead and done it. Maybe she'd really poured that acid on him, just like she said she would.

Then, just for a second, I allowed myself the audacity to believe something hopeful.

Maybe he'd left. Maybe he'd gone back to wherever he came from without a fight because, in a moment of clarity, he remembered we needed that money to live on. Maybe, just this once, he'd decided to be a responsible father.

I caught myself wearing a stupid smirk.

Just like in every thriller movie, the calm didn't last.

I heard the sliding glass door screech open, slow and steady, grinding over tiny, dusty rocks caught in the track until it slammed against the metal stop. Still no yelling. No screaming.

Nothing.

Maybe he's gone, I thought. Maybe she just stepped outside to smoke a cigarette.

I turned to climb back into bed, then froze halfway.

I did a quick Michael Jackson crotch grab to check the stash hiding in the front of my little white Fruit of the Looms. Still there. Whew!

I tucked Dion back in nice and tight and told him to close his eyes and go to sleep.

KaBAM!

The sharpest, loudest slam I'd ever heard shook the walls like an earthquake. At the same time, the radio blasted to full volume, Patrice Rushen singing the end of *"Forget Me Nots."*

My baby sister screamed out, raw and piercing, so my body reacted before my mind could catch up.

That little bit of money I was hiding was everything. Rent. Lights. Food. Diapers.

I couldn't let him find it. I just couldn't.

My head filled with questions all at once.

What if I dropped it?

What if he saw it?

How would we eat?

What about the electricity?

Where would we live if we couldn't pay the rent?

I kicked the covers off, yanked the money from my underwear, and shoved it into my pillowcase. I was going to have to step onto the battlefield.

Maybe this would be the night he finally beat me the same way he beat Mom. Maybe he'd beat me for helping her, or maybe he just wouldn't love me anymore.

On the days he didn't drink, he rubbed my feet and ears to

warm them if they were cold. He made popcorn with a little Lawry's sprinkled on top while we watched *Star Trek* together.

Sometimes we played barbershop, and sometimes he climbed into my bed and sang me to sleep. None of that would happen anymore if I lost him; all of that would be gone.

"Anymore" was a terrifying word for a little boy, but I didn't have time to sit with it.

I had to go help Brianna.

# STALEMATED

*I* hated leaving Dion alone, but Brianna needed me.

I slipped out of my room and across the hall to my baby sister, moving like a nervous thief in a museum. I closed her door behind me.

The room was pitch-black, so I couldn't see the step stool in front of the crib. It was closer than I expected. I tripped and went down hard, my face crashing straight into the plastic bars.

Brianna screamed. This time, it was my fault she was scared.

Dazed and ignoring the sting, I stepped onto the stool and gently lifted her into my arms. I bounced her softly for a moment, then set her at the top end of the crib and tucked blankets around her—just in case the boundaries of this inevitable home boxing match shifted off course.

All their other fights had a soundtrack. Colorful street language, the moans and grunts that went with slaps, kicks, punches, and scratches. But I heard nothing.

I cracked the door and pressed myself against the wall, sliding slowly down the hallway toward their bedroom and the dining room. The 102.3 KJLH night DJ came on and introduced another song.

Still nothing.

No swearing.

No slaps.

No punches.

*Oh my God. She's killed him!*

*Is that how acid works?*

*Or, maybe he killed her.*

With no choice left, I broke out, down the rest of the hall.

I found them crouched in the corner of the dining room, tangled together like two hermit crabs fighting over the same shell. My mother and father had their arms and legs locked around each other, using the walls as leverage. They pressed one another back and forth against the adjoining corners. Their breathing was fierce and ragged, like two lions battling over the carcass of a dead gazelle. Their eyes bulged, wild and ravenous with rage.

Locked in a stalemate.

To each other, they behaved like fearsome opponents, but to me, they were still my mommy and my daddy, and I loved them both.

Dianna's right hand was clenched around Big Paul's Adam's apple, forcing his head back against the wall. Her knuckles were red from squeezing with everything she had. I couldn't see her left hand—it was buried deep in his afro.

My dad's tank top had been ripped open, untucked, and shredded down the front. One of his shoes was missing. I spotted it behind them, abandoned near the kitchen sink.

Paul's right hand was wrapped completely around Dianna's throat. His left fist was locked into her hair, gripping nearly all of her once-perfect curls like he planned to pull every strand straight from her scalp.

Then Dianna started kicking him in the balls, fast and steady, like a jackrabbit.

Still, no one said a word—only muffled grunts, the wet sound of gulping, and the heave of desperate breathing.

Breaking through the quiet, my dad released a long, low growl.

Slowly, and with deliberate force, he straightened his body. Rising into a tall, towering figure over her, he yanked his hand from her hair and tore the front of her nightgown clean open. The fabric split down the middle, exposing her breasts before she could even react. Not to be outdone, she began punching and slapping the daylights out of his face.

Then he snapped both hands around her neck.

His fingers locked there, certain to silence her—and he lifted her.

Up.

And up.

And up.

Her head crept closer to the ceiling, inch by inch, until instinct finally overrode fear, and I knew—*this is too far*. Before my thoughts could catch up, I screamed.

"Stop it! You guys, stop it! PLEASE stop it! Brianna's crying—please, please stop!"

Nothing.

It was like I wasn't even there.

They didn't pause to tell me to leave the room. Didn't shout at me to shut up. They didn't acknowledge me at all.

"Daddy, let her go!"

Nothing.

"Mommy, please stop hitting him!"

She didn't even look at me.

He was tall and strong, with long arms and legs built for leverage. If he kept lifting her like that, she'd be pressed into the corner where the wall met the ceiling, hanging there by his hands alone.

He took his time with it—sliding her body slowly up the dining room wall.

With his hands now locked around her throat, he didn't have to hear her words anymore. For once, the truth attached to her voice didn't matter.

Sure enough—just like I feared—he let out a sharper, higher-pitched growl, and then, *zip*, just like that, she was completely off the floor.

Her head hovered only inches from the ceiling now. Her face flushed deeper and deeper red as her feet kicked helplessly at the air.

She swung her fists wildly, landing blow after blow against the locked hinge of his elbow, but it didn't slow him down. Her movements grew frantic, her breaths now ragged and gasping.

My father didn't flinch.

A strange calm settled over his face—a smugness, almost. The kind that spreads when someone realizes they've won. He looked like the cat who ate the canary, and from the way he held her there, it was clear he didn't give two shits.

Her nightgown, made of white flannel, patterned with tiny pink garden roses, hung torn and crooked from her shoulders now. Green vines connected the little flowers, delicate and cheerful in a way that felt cruel against what was happening. The puffed sleeves were pleated, ending in ruffled cuffs trimmed with lace that peeked out at her wrists. White buttons on what used to be the frilled neckline were all popped off and dotted across the floor.

She could have been Laura Ingalls Wilder if she had the matching bonnet.

That was before.

Now the fabric was ripped and twisted, stained and ruined, and the buttons that once held it together were now popped off and dotted across the dining room floor.

All I could think was that if she died like this, I'd see her forever wearing that gown—her ghost trapped in it—coming back to haunt me for not stopping my dad from killing her right there, in that narrow space where the dining room and living room collided.

This wasn't a fair fight anymore.

Somehow, in my mind, it had always been my job to decide when the line had been crossed. When things tipped from bad into unforgivable. And this—*this*—was it.

I had to do something now, before he accidentally killed her with Dion and Brianna right there in the house.

# BREAK IT BROKEN

My grandparents left their fireplace tools behind when they moved into their new apartment, so I ran past the two of them, into the living room.

The chimney brush?

The shovel?

The poker?

I needed something serious, so I grabbed the heavy iron poker.

Running back, I yelled, "Daddy! Let Mommy go or I hit you with this poker."

Silence.

I waited a few seconds, then climbed onto a dining room chair and gripped this weapon the way I'd learned to hold a baseball bat on the playground.

"Let her go now, Daddy—please!"

I raised the metal rod over my head, teeth clenched, begging myself to wait just one more second. Then another. Trying to believe he would let go.

Another second passed. Then another.

I couldn't wait any longer.

I swung downward with everything I had, like I was He-Man using the power of Grayskull, and hit him square on the back of the head.

On TV, I'd heard parents say right before a spanking, *This is going to hurt me more than it hurts you.*

That night, I finally understood what that meant.

Hitting my father like that split me open to my core—but it worked.

Instantly, my mother was released.

She collapsed onto the floor, eyes squeezed shut, one hand clutching her throat, the other reaching out for me. The coughing. The hacking. The awful sounds she made burned themselves into my memory—sounds I still wish I could forget.

Even now, when I hear a stranger coughing, I am taken back to that night.

It sounded like she was going to die right there on that overly vacuumed, forest-green-and-lime-colored shag carpet, right there in front of me.

My dad collapsed shoulder-first into the wall and slid down fast, his arm stretched out in front of him, frozen. He was defending himself from me, his own son, his namesake.

He didn't look slick anymore. The confusion spread across his face, cutting through the redness in his eyes, made him look like a man snapped out of a spell—like someone waking from possession in the middle of the grimmest fairytale.

I tried to jump down from the chair, but it tipped before I could get my feet under me. I fell over, my head hitting the floor between my mother on the right and my father on the left.

I must have hit it hard because everything went quiet.

At first, there was nothing. I was dangling in the distance. Then a faint ringing, like it was coming from another house, another street. Slowly, my hearing crept back, the way it does when you wake up from a deep sleep and the world hasn't decided to let you back in yet.

The radio was still blasting. Cameo was singing *Back and Forth*.

Brianna was screaming.

Dion was crying.

I forced myself up. I knew that someone would get hurt if we were all in one room together.

I helped my corral mom into her bedroom and shoved the dresser in front of the door, the same way we'd done before, because there *had* been a before. And another before that. Not quite this bad—but close enough.

Okay. Think.

First: call 911.

Then: move the phone out of reach.

Leave it off the hook.

That way, the operator could hear everything. Track the call, and send someone.

I dialed fast. I pressed the phone base against the wall and pulled the receiver as far away as the cord would let it stretch— just far enough to make it harder to hang up.

"You fucking bitch!"

My dad was back on his feet.

And he was pissed.

My dad was yelling, but I couldn't tell who he was yelling at— my mom or me. It didn't matter. If we were going to survive this night, he had to get the hell out of the house.

My mom yanked the dresser away from the door and ran down the hall toward Brianna's room. I followed her.

That's where my dad was now.

He was tearing the room apart—books ripped from shelves, diapers scattered, drawers dumped. He was flipping through book pages like money might be hiding inside the words themselves. He was looking for the cash, obviously, but he was so high it didn't register that our baby sister was still screaming in her crib, and her cries didn't slow him down.

My mom grabbed Brianna, still wrapped in the blanket I'd tucked around her earlier. When she handed her to me, I ran to my room. Brianna's cries had gone hoarse now—laboring, cracked, coated with desperation. The sound scraped at something inside me.

No baby on earth should ever have to cry like that.

If he had reached the point of tearing through books and diapers, my room was next.

I pulled Dion out of bed and opened the closet with one hand. "Get in," I whispered. I passed Brianna to him. "Hold her head up. Be still. And stop crying."

I slid the closet door almost shut—just a crack.

Then I dove onto my bed.

Panic hit all at once. I shoved my arm into the pillowcase, digging frantically for the roll of money. My hand scraped fabric, seams, air—

There it was. I put the roll in my undies and took a deep breath.

Relief came in a quick, sharp pulse—but it didn't last.

*PSSSHHHHHH!*

Something slammed into the wall.

Coins exploded across the other room, clattering and bouncing everywhere.

Brianna's piggy bank.

It was shaped like a little train. Pink. In the window sat a smiling conductor—a girl with pigtails, blue overalls, a yellow shirt—waving as if she'd just won a million dollars.

Now she was shattered into a million-bazillion pieces.

*Wham!*

My parents crashed through my doorway and hit the floor hard.

My mother landed on top of him, fists raised like a boxer at the heavy bag—only this time, my father's head was the target. I flung the closet door open, knowing that if they slammed into it, it would come down on my brother and sister.

Then something happened that still feels unreal.

Dion stepped out calmly.

He was holding Brianna in his arms, gentle, firm, steady. He wasn't crying. Neither was she.

He looked at our parents with a quiet, adult disgust, like someone embarrassed by behavior that had gone too far.

I stepped in front of him immediately, arms out, shielding him.

My dad pushed himself upright. My mom scooped up the baby. Dion and I each grabbed one of my father's legs and started pulling, stomping on his feet.

"Geeeeet oooooout!" Dion screamed.

Get out! Get out! Get out!

The chant took hold of me.

Get out! Get out!

*Bloop...*

The money fell out of my underwear.

"Hand me that money, son."

Time froze—just for a millisecond.

"No."

Daddy charged like a linebacker, as I snatched the roll and dove under the bed, sending him into a frenzy.

I was still small enough to move easily beneath the wooden frame. Even though he was high, even after I'd cracked his skull open, he was careful not to hurt me.

Instead, he reached for me in a way that almost felt playful.

The fire in his eyes was dimmed. In its place, there was something lighter. To my relief, there was no fuming rage or smoldering anger—my father wasn't trying to hurt me. He had never intentionally harmed me before. Not ever. Not even on this night, the night his own son smashed his head in.

From under the bed, I saw Dion and my mom scramble away, down the hall. Then I heard them.

The sirens were growing louder—no longer distant, but close enough to make the windows hum, and my heart race.

My dad shot to his feet and ran out of the room.

I rushed to the toy box and shoved the roll of money deep inside, burying it beneath action figures, trucks, and stuffed animals. Then I sprinted into the living room.

There he was, pacing back and forth like a track star about to get in the blocks. Eyes wild.

"Go get me a clean shirt!" he barked.

The sirens were screaming now.

My mother went and got him one.

She threw a white undershirt at his chest.

"Here. Now get the fuck out!"

She handed me Brianna. I pulled Dion close, and we collapsed onto the sofa together, the three of us pressed into one small knot of fear.

The stereo was still blasting, unbearably loud.

My dad yanked off his torn, bloody tank top, held it against his hip with one hand while the other stroked his goatee—eyes locked on the front window.

Blood slicked his hair, dark and shiny like oil, then trickled down his neck toward his shoulders.

My eyes filled for the first time that night.

I did this to him.

But there was no room for tears.

I straightened my spine and held my breath the way I always did—slow, steady, silent. If I breathed wrong, Brianna might feel it, then start screaming again. We were all holding our breath together now.

The whole house waited.

"Just leave out the back!" my mother screamed.

Paul ripped off his blood-soaked tank top and flung it at her face.

That was all it took.

She snatched the fireplace poker from the floor. That's when he laughed at her—loud, ugly, daring her to use it.

"Ahhh-ha!"

She swung at him, clanging against the metal *Birds in Flight* wall decoration over the sofa, making it sing out like a struck guitar. With another swing, the little San Francisco cable-car salt and pepper shakers exploded across the room in a spray of black and white shards.

My dad spun and bolted. The front door flew open so hard that one of the diamond-shaped panes shattered.

For half a second, he hesitated.

Then he ran into the night, into whatever waited for him out there, increasing the chances of being shot to death right in front of my eyes.

Dianna froze, then let out a raw, animalistic scream. "Moth-afucker!"

She chased him, nightgown torn and hanging off her shoulders, breasts exposed, bare feet slapping pavement. I lay Brianna on the couch and ran after her.

Two squad cars screamed in from opposite ends of Chanslor Street, red and blue lights tearing the darkness apart. Neighbors spilled out of their houses like moths to a flame.

Phillip, Randy, Clark, Reggie.

Faces I knew too well.

That's when Randy's voice cut through everything, sharp and jovial.

"Dang! Is that yo' daddy?"

"Run, nigga, nigga, nigga!"

A rage rose in me all at once.

"Shut up, Randy!"

I yelled—voice cracking.

My parents were halfway down the street, about to cut a hard right at the end of the block. Dianna didn't slow.

She threw the poker into the air and caught it like a javelin, took three calculated steps, and sent it flying.

It struck him square in the back of the neck.

He dropped.

For one frozen second, it looked like the police would have him.

But he was already scrambling up, charging straight toward them.

Panting like a Lioness, Dianna tried to cover herself while staggering back to the front door.

"Boy, get back in the house!"

"Daddy!" I called out. I was sure this would be the last time that I would see him alive, so I risked whatever would happen to me by running down into the street.

"Get your ass in the house!"

"But they're gonna kill him, mommy!"

"Get in the house and shut the curtains."

Through the sheer curtains, I watched, petrified. My father ran back toward the house, head-on into the scrum of fight-ready officers. He took on several with his bare hands, so they fought him with their fists like they had been itching all week for a brawl just like this to go down. Two on one, then three on one, then someone holding him by the arms until he flung himself loose. They kicked him, he kicked back, they punched him, he punched back harder.

I thought that it wouldn't be too much longer until I heard it—

the shot. The one that would kill him, so I covered my ears with my palms as I watched.

The fight lasted only about three minutes, but for two minutes and around twenty seconds, he was whoopin' their asses until they stun gunned him, which put him down right away.

So, they cuffed him in an instant, and Boy, how they show-boated after that. They high-fived and whoop-whooped quite a bit after that, like they really did something great.

I guess they showed him. And I guess that after all, they did do something great. The shackles got squeezed around his wrists tight enough to make him let out a great "Ahh!".

Found in one of my journals from much later on, I wrote: *I must have been thinking, he can't use his hands for anything now. Not for punching or choking, not for holding or tickling. Not for bad, not for good. What about his veins? They stick out a lot. Would the handcuffs cut off his circulation because his veins stick out a lot? Maybe I should tell them because I'm the one who knows this. I'm the only one who really knows because I'm the one who always traces the veins on his wrist with my finger.*

*When we're watching David Carradine on Kung Fu or Captain Kirk on Star Trek, that's when I get a chance to do it. That's when I outline his veins and his knuckles, too. I count how many lines there are in the creases, then I count them on my knuckles too. I wonder how many creases I'll have, and will my knuckles be as strong as his? That's when I use my fingernail to scrape the little bit of dirt out from under his finger-nail while I say stuff to him like, "Daddy, you need to wash your hands."*

*I'd wrap my whole hand around one of his fingers and squeeze hard, wondering if my fingers will ever grow big like this, too. I know what his hands look like when they are clean or dirty, in a mean fist or flat and smooth. I know the whooshing sound they make when he rubs them together before we say grace when we eat, too. But now I've waited too long. They've thrown him head first into the back seat of their car, so my chance at trying to save him is now gone. So is he. Gone, gone, gone.*

"Look at me!" My mother said.

"Paulie, look at me!" I was stuck there, on stupid, staring out the window.

"Take your brother and sister into my bedroom and watch TV."

"Don't come out until I come get you."

"Okay, Mommy."

# 1388 MURCHISON AVE. APT #2

"Mom, Mommy, Mom! "
"What?"
"Why did we move here if there's no grass growing?" "Is it because the trees are blocking the sun, or because this dirt is so old?"
"I don't know, probably both."
"It just looks like gray dust to me! What if we put seeds in the dirt and water them?"
"The landlord is supposed to do that."
"Well, why doesn't he?"
"She's a she, and I guess it's because she doesn't care."
"Well, I care..."
We moved into apartment number two, right next to Ora Lee and Ross, who lived in Number One with their two sons. Brian, a grade below me, had an oddly selfish streak for an oldest child, and Brandon, in the same grade as Dion, who usually behaved like a horny old man with a fascination for playing with matches.

Whatever they overheard drifting from their parents' bedroom, or whatever experiments they tried out in the field when no one was looking, they were more than happy to share. Honestly, it was a bit of a relief knowing they knew what I knew.

Their family came from Mississippi and brought with them an accent that was pure music—soft inflections and relaxed slang that curled around my ears so sweetly and boldly that I couldn't help but mimic it.

I loved the way it sounded like the truth all the time. It made me feel good, grounded, connected to something new that my family usually looked down on.

As long as my grandmother wasn't within earshot, I was free to "Mmm-hmm, child," and "naw, mane," and "I'm fince to" right along with my new friends.

Ora Lee had a sister named Annie Birdsong, with a tattoo on her left shoulder written in a shaky-looking cursive, as if it happened one night on a drunken dare.

The letters were too thick, so they all scrunched together in a blur. The line over the letter T was intentionally slanted, and the dot over the letter I resembled an accent.

You had to be someone she allowed close enough to see it, but once you did, it was clear that it read Latrice—her daughter.

They both lived next door, too. Annie was quiet, smooth-moving, not easily ruffled—a Southern woman with shiny black skin and a bright smile.

Annie drank her tall cans out of a paper bag, neatly folded at the top. She puffed on Kool's while eating Poly Seeds, discreetly spitting the shells into a red plastic cup.

The twin avocado-green buildings we lived in faced each other, four one-story apartments on each side. There was nothing impressive about them. There wasn't even a sign—no *Green Gardens* or *Avocado Courts.*

If there ever had been one, it must have disintegrated into the gray dust we called a courtyard. The small black numbers—1388 —hung crookedly on one building. The other didn't have numbers at all, and since I wasn't allowed past the apartments, I never knew if it was 1386 or 1390.

The front entry was barren, fronted by a tan, cinderblock wall with openings on both sides. Three large, flat-topped boulders sat next to what was probably once a hedge of some kind. Now, it was just a worn-out skeleton of twisted, cracked branches—like someone's dead arms sticking out of frozen quicksand.

A narrow sidewalk wrapped around a dusty courtyard where four massive trees stood in a straight line. In Pomona, we called them Caterpillar trees. Their pale green leaves were nearly as big as your head, billowing together into a thick canopy that muffled the steady hum of the 10 freeway behind the ivy-covered wall across the street. Beneath them, I felt hidden. Safe.

At the back, closest to the alley, were the laundry rooms with one washer, one dryer, and the hot water heater for that row of apartments. Both buildings had a four-space carport facing the alley, and on the other side of the alley was what we called the "old apartments".

An entire neighborhood of condemned, graffiti-covered, boarded-up apartment buildings on the left, the right, and all behind us. The whole area felt like a ghost town, and there we were, right in the middle of it, waiting to be next.

"I don't want to see you over there in those apartments, you hear me?"

"Yes, but, what happened to them?"

"Everybody moved out."

"Why'd they move?"

"Because they're condemned."

"Okay."

Usually, when I got a brick wall kind of response like that, I took it as a hint to shut the hell up. I figured I'd find out the dirt from the other kids anyway.

White signs with red letters—NO TRESPASSING, California

Penal Code 602—were stapled and nailed to broken doors and window frames.

Shards of glass glittered in the dirt where flower beds had once been. The walkways sparkled like mirrors turned toward the sun. It was the closest thing to a war zone I had ever seen, and yet I was drawn to it by the *yester-what* of it all.

I was fascinated by the leftover ghosts of the people who once lived there, the lives they had led, the stories they might have told.

I imagined children dressed like Dracula, witches, and mummies, once knocking at these doors—yelling out Trick or Treat.

On Thanksgiving, you could smell the faint scent of turkey and Mama's sweet potato pie emanating from any open space between windows or door cracks.

An overused, garland-wrapped wreath hung at the door during Christmas time, with the tree visible from outside, all lit up and dancing with tinsel whenever the kids brushed by.

Now it was just a shithole, and no one gave a shit, so the shit that once happened there wasn't worth remembering for shit. It looked like shit, but nobody complained about the shit because our rent was cheap as shit, so the shit just stayed looking like shit.

Nobody ever explained why either. We didn't need them to. As street-smart kids, we chalked it up to the Holy Trinity of the hood: crack, gangs, and violence. No fact-checking required. That was it.

So, in true urbanite fashion, we made the best of it. We checked that we weren't being watched and used that ghost town as a secret playland. Bouncing on old, dirty mattresses and building forts out of punched-out closet doors. Like my mom said, she didn't want to *see* me playing in there.

On a warm, clear day, soon after we moved in, I had just put our clothes in the washer and placed the yellow plastic hamper on top of the machine.

Walking out to the alley, I wanted to see if anyone else was outside playing when I heard, "Hey, you wanna play doin' it to my baby?"

I blurted out, "Doin' it to my what?" and then, after putting together exactly what I had heard, I whispered, "Where are you?"

Following the sound to the front of the carport, I found Brandon hiding underneath the overhanging storage cabinets. Every bit of six years old, going on sixteen, pressed up against the grill of somebody's green Pinto. Pants unbuttoned, wiener out, grinding against the car.

"What are you doing? "I hissed frantically. "You're gonna get caught!"

From around the wall, like gibbons escaped from the zoo, Jesus, the boy from apartment number four on our side, and Brian, joined in—ceremoniously mounting the front of the car with Brandon like they had all done this before.

They awkwardly began their juvenile interpretation of manly grunts and humping motions while singing in rhythm, "doin' it to my baaaby, doin' it to my baaaby."

I froze. My first instinct was shock, but like any boy in a group, I was not going to be outdone.

I looked out to see if any adults were around, then bolted right on over to join them.

Jesus laughed, then turned to me with this big Howdy Doodie grin and said, "This is my dad's car!" Amused and confused, I asked, "Then why are you laughing?"

Let's get a couple of things straight here. I did not do the chant, and I did not undo my pants. No way!

That was a little too bold for me. Mostly, I just wanted to see the other guy's wieners anyway.

Besides, if we got caught, I was *not* going to be *that* guy when the parents told one another the embarrassing true story about the time all those nasty ass little boys got caught humping

Jesus's daddy's green Pinto in the carport with their wieners out.

Brandon looked over at Jesus and whispered, "Why does yours look like that?" Everybody stopped humping and looked.

"Like what, stupid?"

"You can't see where you pee from. Why is it like that?"

Jesus shrugged, "I don't know, dude, maybe it's cause I'm Mexican!"

Brandon shrugged, then we all looked at each other and shrugged.

I whispered nervously, "I hear someone coming."

"Cowabunga!" Brian yelled. And just like that, we scattered in every direction, zipping up and running, turning our little carport scandal into a blur of legs and laughter.

After our toxic male triste with the Pinto, Latrice emerged. Taller than the other boys and sweet, like how all the little girls back then were required to be. She always said please and thank you, and smiled when she was supposed to.

We were the same height, which, amongst kids, automatically makes you equals. We both loved J.J. Fadd, Salt n Peppa, and Soul II Soul.

She had cocoa butter smooth, dark chocolate skin, and gleaming white teeth that were just a little crooked with a gap between the front two.

Square faced with a sharp jawline, tiny little ears pierced with gold gumdrop studs—her hair was always parted into three sections: two on the side and one in the back, each one tied into a loop with a click-clack to match her outfit.

Latrice carried herself with the poise of someone already sure of the world, even at our age.

One day, while the rest of the kids were somewhere else, Duck Tales was on TV in the background. Sitting crisscross applesauce on the floor of Brian and Brandon's room while facing one another, Latrice was teaching me how to play Pitty-Pat like a Vegas pro.

"Everybody gets five cards." She said.

"O.K."

"The rest go into the middle, then the first player flips over the up card."

"The up card?"

"Yeah, flip the top card over and put it on the side."

"Like that?

"Yeah. You really never played this ba'foe?"

"No."

"Do you have any matches?"

"Yeah."

"Put 'em on top, boy."

"Like that?"

"Yeah, now discard."

"What's that?

"Ntch." She sucked her teeth a little.

"Pick a card out of yo' hand that you think I cain't match, then throw it down, face up on the side pile."

"Okay. Like that?"

"Yeah, like that. And quit sayin' like that."

We laughed as she lightly bopped my head with the tip of her cards. She had something to tell me.

"Child, guess what?"

"Girl, what?"

"My mamma done come home from Newberry's today with a big bag full of stuff."

"What stuff?"

"I'm finna tell you! My mama said, girl, you gon' have to wear these here training bras cause yo' titties startin' to come in."

My mouth dropped as I stuck my neck out and squinted my eyes while she poked out her chest.

"I don't see any boobs," I said very candidly.

"Well, they comin', I can feel 'em, too."

My face now scrunched up, I said, "What does it feel like?"

"Like there's a bump underneath on both sides, and it hurts a little, but like a weird hurt. Here, feel."

As I reached out with my four fingers, she grabbed my hand to place it in the right spot. I felt it just like she said, too. It was a bump, alright.

"Ewww," I said, my lips still turned up. "Is it gonna stay like that?"

"No fool, they turn into real titties one day. Then her eyes froze as she had a revelation.

"Lawd, I jus' hope not as big as Ora Lee and my Mamas, though!"

She shook her head, eyes looking at the floor. "They titties go from here, all the way to across the street!"

As we cackled in high-pitched laughter. I screamed out, "Across the street!"

I laughed like a drunken fool while Latrice egged me on— miming the shape of huge titties in front of herself with her arms.

Tears flowed down our cheeks as we both oooh'd and awed, pressing our hands to our sides while rolling around on the floor in the exquisite joy of laughter and tears.

It was the kind of together laughter that only two young friends could understand. The blissful kind that binds you to a moment for a lifetime.

We composed ourselves like the way we figured grown-ups must do, and reorganized the cards in our hands, while we repositioned our butts to sit up straight, and cleared our throats.

Latrice reared her head back, grimaced, and said dryly, "Thought I was supposed to git titties first, *then* my monthly visitor."

"Did you?"

"Did I what?"

"Start your period?"

"Child, yes!"

Leaning in, she whispered as if we were in a room filled with nosy people.

"But I use pads because my mama said tampons are for fast girls, tramps, and hoes."

I nodded as if I were an expert on the topic, then confided in her, "My mom uses pads too. Sometimes I have to go get them for her at the seven-eleven, and guess what?"

"Oooh, what?"

"My best friend at school, Melissa, started her period during lunch recess the other day." (Latrice was my "at-home" best friend.)

"Fa real?" She said while rearranging the cards in her hand.

"Mm Hmm, girl." "We were sitting in the grass with some other girls, and I saw a red spot getting bigger and bigger, so I gave her my jacket to wrap around her waist, and then I told her, 'I think you started your period."

Looking over the top of her cards, Latrice asked, "What did she do?"

"She started crying."

Latrice pressed her lips together hard, then asked, "Wha's her name?"

"Melissa," I said, like she should already know.

"That big, tall white girl you always wit' at recess?"

"Yeah."

"What was she cryin' fa'? It don't hurt when you *first* git it."

"I don't know, I guess she was just scared."

She popped her lips really loud, "Well, I guess," she said, rolling her eyes as she smacked her cards down one after the other from her hand.

She closed her eyes, tilted her head to one side, snapped her fingers, and called out, "Pitty- Pat! I win chile'."

Latrice was only shy in front of adults and strangers. With me, she was all candor and nerve, saying exactly what she meant about things that stayed between us. From her, I learned that honesty—especially about the practical, awkward parts of life—was one of the quiet, magical threads that stitched people like us together.

We played whenever we could, and we never disagreed like all the other kids did. If neither of us had caught the ice cream truck in a few days, we'd make a Chinese jump rope out of rubber bands instead.

The fancy kind cost twenty-five cents from the ice cream man, or a dollar at the Seven-Eleven plus tax, but getting it meant crossing the empty field where a little girl named Casey had been kidnapped. So we usually said, forget that.

We might get in trouble for using up all the rubber bands, but it was faster, cheaper, and safer just to make one.

Besides, Big Head Brian would eventually find a way to steal it, shoot it up a tree, bury it, or throw it over the wall onto the freeway anyway.

Once, Ora Lee let us hold him down and pop the naps out of his hair with a metal comb for stealing our rope.

Latrice and I would sit in the grass behind the patios, in the shade, looping the rope together two rubber bands at a time. We'd wrap it around a tree so one of us could hold it around our legs while the other jumped.

The younger girls mostly watched as we taught them the steps. We didn't even bother asking the boys to play—"They too stupid to even hold the rope, anyway!" Latrice would say.

On Saturdays, after breakfast and the sacred lineup of morning cartoons, we'd meet outside to play school. Shaquailia from apartment three came, along with Tamara and Destiny from the other building. They were younger, so naturally, we were in charge.

"Good morning, class. My name is Mrs. Birdsong," Latrice would announce every Saturday like it was the first day of school.

"Good morning, Mrs. Birdsong."

"This is your principal, Mr. Whitmore," she'd say, pointing to me.

"Good morning, Mr. Whitmooooore," they'd sing back, giggling.

"Please stand for the Pledge of Allegiance."

They'd carefully set their folders and pencils beside them, smiling as they stood—that was usually when the boys showed up.

"Go back over there!" One of us would shout. "Leave us alone!"

Latrice echoed, waving her prized Garfield-and-Odie ruler from the book fair.

Here came the boys—my hard-headed brother Dion, Brian, Jesus, and the rest of them—storming over like Lord of the Flies, ready to wreck whatever peaceful moment we'd built.

"We been in school all week," they'd say. "Now y'all wanna play it at home, too?" "Y'all stupid!"

Someone from our side would say, "You said you didn't wanna play, fool!"

If you wanted to turn sweet Latrice into a monster, this was how you did it. She'd bite her bottom lip, shoulders tightening, then it was on.

"Shut up and get on!"

"Shut don't go up, but prices do, so take my advice and shut up too!"

"Oh, you think you bad now, huh?"

"Yeah, I'm bad!"

"Boy, Imma—"

Latrice bolted after her cousins, while I flattened Dion and Jesus. The sound of her fist hitting Brian's back was a hard, hollow thud, like a rock hitting dirt. He moaned like Bugs Bunny, rolling around trying to shake the sting out of it.

"Let us be!" she yelled. "Go on now, boy, or Imma' smack the tar outta you!"

Her accent came roaring back whenever she was whooping somebody.

After a little begging and a few more swings, we'd let them play with us until the air started to smell like the spices and seasoning of dinner. That's when we would all head back to the courtyard so we were close enough to be seen, as we waited for permission to come inside, wash our faces and hands, sit down at the table, and say grace before we ate.

# NEW FOR A FEW

Our new apartment had brown carpeting, and we painted the living room baby blue. We got brand new furniture from a new place called Remco, where you could do something like a reverse layaway. This place would even have all the stuff delivered to your home before everything was all paid off, which blew my mind.

We got a plush Gray L-shaped sectional sofa set with an oak-like end table topped with a grayish-blue lamp and a white lampshade with the plastic still on it.

The matching coffee table had four square, tinted glass panels in it, easily removable for cleaning purposes—according to the salesman.

The dining room table was a modern-looking off-white with a blueish colored trim around the bottom.

The guy in the store told my mom that it came with a removable leaf for the holidays. This shit was gettin' fancier and fancier by the second.

We found new curtains with ducks wearing blue bonnets to replace the old ones with baskets of strawberries on them.

We had the strawberry curtains all my life, and I loved them, but my mom said they were old-fashioned now, and it was time for something new.

We painted the kitchen wall yellow to match the smiling bills on each of the ducks, so it all looked fresh like the people on TV had.

Everything had decorative flair. You could always trust my mother to do something new. Whether it was fashion, hairstyles, or housewares, she was an innovator who also followed the trends.

The best part of all this newness was the brand-new giant 32" color TV set, on a swivel base. A Swivel for God Sakes! Push buttons on it and everything, with a remote control! A remote control! Man, this was some futuristic shit right here!

The only worrisome part about it was hearing the guy at the store tell my mother that it could all be repossessed if we missed any payments. Just something else for me to worry about.

We got bunkbed frames from a yard sale, but the box springs and mattress were new. Factory fresh with the plastic still on, direct from Discount Furniture Center over on Holt Ave.

This all started to feel too much like a peaceful new beginning, but I knew down deep that it was too good to be true. It always was, anyway. I knew that my dad wasn't coming back to be with us. I just felt it. I also knew that if I let myself believe that everything would always be fine, it would wind up being snatched right from my little hands, beaten to a pulp, then left there at my feet like a dead bird for me to either cry over, bury, or both.

I learned not to get my hopes up too high if I didn't want to be let down hard. That's why whenever Dion asked about Daddy coming back, I just did things like hum the tune to the shape of the words *I don't know*, like a song.

Sometimes I'd respond with maybe, but I never ever said the H word. Not *hopefully*! I absolutely never told him to go ask Mom either. I wasn't about to be the reason for that can of worms being opened. I felt guilty knowing better, though.

I stayed still within my hollow answers, which probably left him more confused, but what could I do? I wasn't in charge.

Didn't he remember all of the fighting? All the blood, the screaming, the hair-pulling between them. What about all the broken glass everywhere?

Our old bunk beds were smashed to bits. What about that? Didn't he remember that? I thought, *just leave it alone.* Quit asking.

Together, our parents were an overflowing Duran and Son's garbage bin doused in kerosene, then set on fire in an alley. Besides, if we wanted to keep all this new furniture nice, it's best to just hope they'll stay apart rather than wishing them back together again. At least until we all grew up and moved out.

I wondered if Dion understood this reality. That we were starting a new, fatherless life. Our mother said she always hoped for us to live in a house with a Cocker Spaniel and a brand-new, modern car. She hadn't said anything about a new man at all.

I just wanted quiet nights watching TV, eating popcorn without peeping over at the window to see if Daddy was coming up the walkway drunk again.

Getting in bed, falling asleep without being woken up to foul-mouthed cursing or the sound of bric-a-brac clacking against the walls.

Or thinking about how many days you'd have to wear your shoes in the house, before all the tiny little broken shards of porcelain were finally all vacuumed up.

Having more than three bath towels, more toilet paper right there under the sink, instead of having to wipe with a wet washcloth.

Another tube of toothpaste when the last one ran out, so we didn't have to endure the bitterness of baking soda until Mom's next county check came.

Dion didn't know. I knew he didn't know. Now and then, I found a paltry little piece of me secretly wishing he did, though.

At least then, I'd have someone to talk to—feel the same feelings with. Maybe I was a little mad at him, too, because when I was his age, I was aware, so why wasn't he?

We were brothers. He should be able to see, too, right? But this new life wasn't registering for him because he was still too new.

# WELL, DAMN...

$\mathcal{I}$n the midst of all this newness, it happened on a Saturday, when Soul Train had just gone off, and Latrice went back home. My mom came into the living room holding a pair of Brianna's little toddler-sized acid-washed jeans to tell us some news.

"Your dad is coming to take you guys to the park, so go get dressed."

Dion and I looked at each other with trepidation. Mostly because we didn't know if we were allowed to be excited, but also because we wondered what the catch was.

"Now?" I said, in disbelief.

"Yes, now. He just called from over at the Seven-Eleven. I told him it was ok for them to head over."

*Them?*

We hadn't seen him in almost a year, so why now? And why did this sound planned? Just when things were starting to feel light again, like spring was finally glowing on our faces, he came knocking—a deadbeat dad back to flex his rights and stir up our little delicate hearts with promises and confusion.

"He said they want to take you guys over to Kiwanis Park, so put on some shorts. Did you hear me?"

"What park?" I said, trying to buy time.

"Boy! Go git dressed!"

I knew exactly what to wear: my new white shorts, my white button-down with the gray Kente-cloth pattern, and my brown belt. I loved that shirt. I wore it for my fourth-grade picture, but Mom had made me put a gray Sasson sweater over it, so all you could see was the collar. I was still mad about that.

I wanted my dad to see the whole shirt.

I wanted him to know I had style. That I could look good even without him teaching me. I wanted him to be proud of all of us— me, Dion, Brianna—to see what he was missing.

Maybe then he'd want to stay.

Then I could crush him by saying something facetious like, *It was nice seeing you, but we don't really need you anymore. Ta-ta for now.* Or maybe, *come on in, it's been so quiet around here without you.* I just wanted him to feel as bad as I had.

I got dressed quickly so that I could help Dion. I picked out a white polo shirt and some navy-blue shorts for him. I usually helped to pick out his clothes. We didn't ever wear matching outfits, but we did have matching blue and white tennis shoes with the Velcro straps, so we wore those.

"Go put on some Sta-Sof-Fro and rub it in good."

"Okay!" Dion was excited, now, boy!

"What's wrong?"

"It won't come out."

"Here." I loosened the cap. "Put a little water in it."

I grabbed the Jergens to lotion his face, elbows, and knees. The mist from the spray bottle fell onto my face and arms.

"Spray your head, not me!" "Rub it in too, so I can comb through it."

After running the natural comb through Dion's hair, I patted down his little afro with salon-like precision, then did the same to my own.

We both looked in the mirror, pointed at ourselves, and said, "Fressshhh!"

My mom put Brianna in a white sundress with strawberry print all over it, and a pair of jeans so that her chunky little legs wouldn't get scratched up in the sand.

"Did you put lotion on?"

"Yes!" We said in unison.

"Go get me the brush and the pink oil. Bring me her rubber bands, too."

She was talking to me. She was always talking to me, even if she didn't specify. If something needed to be gotten, washed, rinsed, folded, stacked, or put back, she was talking to me.

I learned over the years how to avoid any consequences, so I'd snap to it right away. I ran to the bathroom, grabbed Brianna's hair basket with everything in it, and hustled back to the living room.

*Willow* was playing on HBO, so Dion and I sat down in front of it to watch.

"Move back some."

"Okay." We answered together, while shimmying our butts back.

"Here, put this away." I had just sat down, not even two minutes ago, but that's how she kept me jumping.

Instinctually, I sprang right up to get the basket. When I did, I heard the faint twisting of the security screen knob.

Then, the knock against the metal screen door got me right in the heart. It skipped a couple of beats. Those missing beats felt like a sledgehammer had pounded into the place where I put my right hand to say the pledge of allegiance at school. I almost went to put my hand there, but that seemed like something Fred G.

Sanford, pretending to go home to his dead wife Elizabeth, would do.

I just paused right where I stood, and no, Dion wasn't excited anymore.

Caught off guard by the intensity of my fear, my mind played back all the old disaster plans.

Should I get the big knife, so he could fall on her like she used to say to him? Can I grab Brianna fast enough to save her from being kicked across the room the same way I had been before?

What about the acid? Was there any acid? My mind raced through all the schemes my mother would lay out for getting rid of this man, but she was the one who invited him here.

Dion stood up at attention, facing the door, so I went and stood in front of him in case some shit popped off between good ol' Tyson and Holifield.

"Who is it?"

My mother sang the words.

She picked Brianna up from the sofa, then posed her like a Cabbage Patch doll on her hip.

Though I knew better than to show it, my mouth began its slow-motion descent into slack. My entire face was slowly vanquished by a dumbfounded expression over which I had absolutely no control. I was stunned.

"It's me!" My dad called out.

With a coy flirtation and a smile in his voice, even! *What is happening, and who the "F" are these people?*

"Me who?" With a lilt, even.

*Is she kidding me right now?*

Looking back at us, she was smiling. Did she want us to smile, too? I wasn't smiling. I was too busy looking behind me for the Candid Camera crew to pop out.

"Girl, you betta' open this door."

As she reached across the coffee table for her house keys, I held my breath as they glided softly across the brand-new glass panels, easily removable for faster cleaning.

*Is she getting ready to get him in here and beat him to death or something? What the heck is she smiling at?*

She unlocked the door as I grabbed onto Dion's wrist. I waited on high alert. I began squinting and licking my lips like I used to. My top and bottom teeth meet to form that familiar pressure my jaws knew so well.

Old Man Nervousness was back to get me. He was preparing me for the worst, and I had no other friends to tell me what to do, so I did exactly what he said.

Like bacon in a hot frying pan, the muscles in my neck and shoulders began to seize.

When she turned the key in the deadbolt for the final time, I squeezed a little more firmly, causing Dion to look up at me.

"Come in, you look nice." She opened the security screen.

"Hey, there's my babies!" "Daddy missed you!"

Dion darted over like the wind. "Daddy!" *Traitor.*

"Hey Jing-Jing!" "How's my boy?"

"You're gettin' so big."

"Hey! Come over here, Wally Gator." That's what he always used to call me. A gay cartoon alligator

He had a tone in his voice like it was one of those Good Sundays again.

"Hi, Daddy." The words trickled from my lips, hitting the floor like steel marbles.

"What's wrong? Get over here. I haven't seen you in a minute."

Exactly! How could he not know that that was precisely what the fuck was wrong?

"Are we going to the park?" I asked.

"Yeah, man!" "But I have somebody that I want you guys to meet."

*Did he buy us a puppy or something?*

We said, "See you later," to our mother, kissed her as we went out the door, but I couldn't help thinking, why wasn't she coming with us, and who in the world could he possibly want us to meet?

My dad hoisted Brianna up high on his chest, kissing her chunky little cheeks over and over. Dion held his other hand, beaming with joy.

Me? I was watching closely from just a couple of steps behind. That way, I could make sure that he wasn't trying to kidnap us like Latrice said one day before.

"Where y'all's daddy at?"

"He lives at some church thing out by Disneyland."

"Child, don't let him kidnap ya' now."

"What?"

"You know Tiffany Glostin?"

"Yeah, she was in my class last year."

"She told me that after her mama kicked her daddy out, her daddy took her one day to spend the night, and he tried to kidnap her!"

"Pshh, don't worry, that won't happen to us."

"Boy, how you know dat?"

"Because Dion and I lived with our dad right before we moved here, girl. He ain't even want us then."

What she didn't know was that for a few months, my dad was our sole guardian—and boy, oh boy, poor guy, did he fuck that right the hell up.

We lived at our Aunt Diane's house with her and her family out in the city of Los Angeles proper.

We were enrolled at LaSalle Avenue Elementary, a school so violent that lunchtime felt less like a break and more like a prison yard. Every day, as soon as the bell rang for recess, I'd hunt down my brother so we could make our escape.

We'd cut through the neighborhood to a nearby park, claim a picnic table, and eat our brown-bag lunches in peace.

Afterward, we'd play until I heard the final bell echo in the distance. Then we'd pack up and walk home, just as if nothing out of place had happened.

Sometimes, on the walk back, we'd spot our dad coming toward home on the opposite side of the street. We'd shout, *"Daddy! Daddy—over here!"*

Sometimes he heard us. Sometimes he didn't. It depended on whether he was too high, too drunk, or impressively committed to being both at the same time.

On the days he crossed over and walked with us, I felt safe, but still out of place. This safety was only temporary. It was borrowed and liable to be taken back without notice.

That school was so awful that no one ever asked where we went after lunch. Not once. We vanished every day, and the next morning would begin the same as the last, with no mention of our absence, as if it was expected. Like it was normal.

Latrice asked, "When is he comin' to see you again?"

"I don't know… maybe never."

There we were, my two siblings and I, following our dad out to the car, when I noticed a woman sitting in the front passenger seat, fixing her makeup in the sun visor mirror. That's when my dad said, "Okay, Wally, get in."

# THE TORNADO

Standing there at the car door, the very last fight sprang up in my mind. After the very last fight, the night the police took my daddy to jail, we went into hiding, which I thought was stupid because he was in jail already.

And besides, he wasn't coming after us, not like that, anyway. We stayed at my mom's friend Barbara's house for about a week or so, then when we came home, we found what we must have been hiding from, what we wound up calling The Tornado.

Excited to be home and away from Barbara's filthy house and her annoying son, Joey, we pulled up to return home. I guess my mom thought the coast would be clear or that my dad would be in jail still.

Who knows? Shock is the best and plainest way to describe the feeling of coming home to find what we found that day when we made our way into the apartment. We named it The Tornado.

Walking up the grass, hands deep in my pants pockets, I noticed through the screen that the front door was wide open.

We had been robbed many times before, so it didn't faze me much. In our neighborhood, getting robbed was like having to scrape a wad of gum off the bottom of your shoe or having to clean up after somebody vomited on the hot sidewalk.

Sure, it was a nuisance, but the only real thing that pissed you off was the inconsiderate mess that was left behind. If you're gonna steal our shit, at least do it neatly.

One night when we lived in the back apartment, this fool broke in and stole my mother's little red, quilt-pattern wallet.

Then, to add insult to injury, he stole the pot roast my mom had been slow-cooking overnight in the oven. Somehow, we found her wallet outside in the dumpster the next morning, but we sure never saw a single slice of that damn roast.

That was right around the time the Night Stalker was around —Richard Ramirez—breaking into houses, raping, and killing people. Everybody nailed chain-link fencing to the inside of their windows and stacked glasses and bottles on the sills so you'd hear them crash if someone tried to climb in. Coke bottles, wine glasses, beer bottles—anything that would shatter.

Standing side by side with my mother at the front of the apartment, we knew the culprits were probably long gone if the door was open, but just to be safe, my mom and I put Dion and Brianna back in the car anyway.

As we approached, I could hear the sound of something frying on the stove. Then we smelled it.

Potatoes.

My dad's potatoes.

Which meant he was inside.

He must've been high or drunk or somewhere else in his head, thinking it was one of those Good Sundays. Mom and I looked at each other. I was scared, but if I'm being honest, I was also a little excited about the potatoes.

We went inside where we found him standing there in the kitchen, looking like a zombie chef holding a spatula, Daddy was home. Facing away from us in front of the stove, wearing nothing but some baggy white Fruit of the Looms, sporting a lopsided, nappy afro.

Dried streaks of blood covered his dirt-stained body like brown cracks in desert mud.

The state of our little apartment was atrocious. Our jaws dropped at the sight of how blasted everything was.

All the dishes from the cupboards were broken on the floor around him. Mixed among the chunks of what used to be dinner plates, teacups, and cereal bowls were all the forks, knives, and spoons that we ate with.

Everything was everywhere it didn't belong. Pots, pans, lids, mixing bowls, all strewn about, scattered on the floor, and this pitiful man had the nerve to be barefoot.

I felt paralyzed by the volume of disgrace filling the inside of this once always clean, always neat place that we called our home. This used to be Mom-Mom and Pop-Pop's apartment. How could he do this?

I wanted to run away, but my feet felt glued to the white octagonal tiles in the entryway where I had stood so many times before. So, I stood there bravely with my mother, holding her hand a little tighter, pulling back with just enough resistance so that she could understand what I was saying without words— let's go!

Since he hadn't turned around yet, I figured we still had a chance to get the hell outta Dodge without World War III starting up again. That's when my mom reached down and snatched up my grandmother's deviled egg plate from right in front of her feet —the only thing made of glass on the floor that wasn't broken.

She growled at him. "What the fuck is wrong with you, Paul!"

He continued to say nothing. Didn't budge. He just kept stirring those potatoes, his underwear shaking side to side, elastic shot, hole in the right butt-cheek side.

I began to worry about seeing what his face looked like, too. I started to think about how Blackula looked when he got mad. How in all the movies, the stringy hair on Blackula's cheeks just under his eyes would suddenly be there when it wasn't there before, and how his face would get all white and sweaty, his eyes glowing red.

"Hey, I'm talking to you!" Still, she got no response.

"Daddy, we're home,"

Nothing sank, nothing landed; he said nothing. It was like talking to a lampshade with a very high pulse.

Then, out of the corner of my eye, I noticed what happened to the actual lamp shades, along with damn near everything else that we owned.

The wrought-iron etagere was tipped over, caught by the torn arm of the sofa. Every porcelain figurine was pulverized into dust. He must have stomped them. He didn't own tools.

Something inside him had finally split, and no one was there to hold him back so he had screamed all of his screams, and some of mine too. I think even out-screamed all of us with this rampage he went on.

He especially out screamed Dianna for once, and that is why she was silent in this moment. He shut her right the fuck up. After all of her screaming, yelling, picking, and blaming.

That tornado had come out of him and ripped our home apart so bad it could never be put back together again.

I ran through the wreckage. The dining table on its side, the chairs slammed into the walls. Clothes and papers in the hallway.

Our bunk beds were destroyed. Slats splintered. Mattresses ripped open. Springs and stuffing everywhere like snow.

I don't know how he did it.

Brianna's room was mostly untouched, her crib still standing. Maybe something about seeing the baby's things slowed him down.

I wondered whose face he saw as he did all this. Was it only

Dianna's? How about his absentee father, Johnny Estrada, the man he only saw in person two times in his whole life?

What about his grandmother, who raised him since his mother couldn't or didn't want to? Maybe it was all those uncles who put alcohol in his bottle when he was a baby. Or Mom-Mom and Pop-Pop for thinking that he wasn't good enough for their daughter or their grandchildren.

Who knew, and how would we ever know? All I could do was hope, for what I thought to be a selfish reason, that this rage wasn't because of me.

"My bike!" I yelled, running toward the patio in as much of a tizzy as any little boy is allowed to have.

Before reaching the sliding glass door, I saw that my mom had found the broken pieces of her Kwan Yin statue. Protector of women and children.

Paused in time before me, staring up at the ceiling on her knees, while holding the snapped off porcelain base with the bare feet of the goddess still attached.

This was the thing that broke her.

So my mother, Dianna, powerless over the situation, began to cry tears of sadness. Since I knew all about her, I knew all about these kinds of tears of hers, too.

The same tears as when she found out from my very own big mouth that Paul was sleeping with the lady who lived across the street from the Toys R Us.

Big tears with sounds made due to dripping snot, like the night she found out that her best friend, my Aunt Gayle, died because of her cancer.

Knelt down in prayer position on the floor next to her bed, arms stretched out across the gold bedspread with white leaves on it, her hands clasped together while desperately shouting the word "why", and saying, "please God" and "I love you Gayle", over and over again, all night that night.

I could see no angry tears here, not this time. No, this time she hurt. Bad, too, and I knew it because I could feel it with her, every bit of it.

Her spirit ached because she was overtired. Tired of Paul but realizing too how tired she had become with her own choices, she finally decided to do what I had been saying we should do for a long time. Just go.

Clearing her throat, then shaking her head, up she stood, with the deviled egg plate in one hand, she said. "Get in the car."

# NO THANK YOU

"Go ahead, Wally Gator—get in the car."

I was pulled back into the uncomfortable present I'd drifted away from.

"This is who I wanted you to meet. This is Tina—Daddy's new girlfriend."

I wasn't used to him third-personing himself like that. "This is Daddy's new…" anything. Especially not when it referred to some new piece of ass he'd picked up during his born-again phase and his first real attempt at sobriety.

"Say hi," he smiled, nudging the words out of his mouth like a command.

I smiled my words right back at her. "No, thank you."

This very beautiful, slightly sneaky-looking woman jerked her head back and blinked fast, like she'd been slapped with something invisible.

When she stepped out of the car, she was almost a mirror image of my mother. I was perplexed—but she'd never get the chance to know it. She was younger than my mom. Too young.

Definitely too young to be the girlfriend of a grown man with three kids.

Her eager expressions made her look dimmer than the adults I was used to, and the resemblance to Dianna was so strong it tipped into something unsettling.

If he wanted something different, why had he found a clone? It was like watching a Scooby-Doo villain show up wearing my mother's body as a costume. I wanted to rip the mask off and see what kind of ugly was underneath.

That revelation would come soon enough.

Dianna's father was Italian; her mother was Black. Her skin was light, with a sun-kissed olive shine. Her heart-shaped face was framed by long, dark hair. She wore fitted cotton-nylon dresses with bold prints, cinched at the waist with wide belts, matched to extra-high heels.

She had all the curves men like, and a booty that could stop traffic—or at least slow it down enough for otherwise polite men to start with, "Hey baby," or "Mmm-mmph!"

When they were bold enough, they'd call out, "Come ova here, lemme holla atcha, sweet thang," from across Dudley Street or outside the Top Hat Liquor Store.

"Ignore them," she'd say, cool as ever.

And we would—backs straight, shoulders set, noses tilted high as we glided past. We'd sing the *Laverne & Shirley* theme song as we strutted away, proving just how little of her attention they had.

Tina looked like that woman—but she wasn't that woman.

Where Dianna was cool and sure, Tina was tight and shifty. Her eyes slid around when she talked, like she was always checking to see who was watching. I rolled my eyes so hard they almost hurt. My instincts had never been wrong about bad grown-ups, and this one felt wrong.

"Do you want to sit in the front with your dad?" she asked.

"It's not safe for kids to sit in the front."

"I can hold Brianna on my lap."

"She doesn't like strangers."

"I think she'll be okay."

"No, she wouldn't."

I motioned Dion into the back seat, took Brianna from my father, buckled us in together, and stared at Tina through the side mirror until she finally looked away. Any grown-up who tried to out-stare a kid was suspect to me.

The park was only a short drive around the corner, over on Weber Street. Once we arrived, Tina jumped out of the front seat with her arms stretched out, hoping to grab Brianna. I moved fast, hustling the kids over to the swing set. There was one of those baby swings, so I strapped Brianna in and gave her a push. That kept us occupied—and kept us away from "you-know-who" for the moment.

Dion and I ran around, taking turns on the jungle gym and swinging Brianna. We made faces, told jokes, and ran in circles to make her laugh. Meanwhile, the "lovebirds" sprawled a blanket in the shade, unpacked the trunk, and placed each item with precise, annoying neatness.

After a while, Daddy yelled, "Hey, guys, come see what we got!" I grabbed Brianna out of the swing and raced over.

From a plastic bag, he pulled out a mini football for Dion, a knock-off Barbie for Brianna, and a see-through green water gun for me.

Then came the feast of 7-11 ham and cheese sandwiches wrapped in plastic, a bag of Cool Ranch Doritos, Jello pudding packs, and root beers to wash it all down.

"We're not allowed to drink soda; it gives you cavities," I said firmly.

"Well, we won't tell your mom if you don't," Tina said, trying to win me over.

I squinted at her. "I have to tell my mom everything; she's my mom."

"Okay, have a sandwich," she said, sounding slightly irritated.

"I'll just have pudding. Where are the spoons?"

"Oh no! We must have forgotten the spoons, Wally," Dad chimed in, trying to smooth things over.

"I'll just have Doritos, Daddy. May I have a napkin, please?"

"Oh no, Paulie, I think we forgot the napkins."

*Wait—did she just call me Paulie?*

I glared at her. "Only my family calls me Paulie. Other people call me Little Paul. You should call me Little Paul."

Instantly, I hated her. With the fake smile, the false sweetness, and the "I'm good with kids" act, I knew exactly what she was doing: impressing Dad. The only thing he cared about was that she looked like Dianna and… functioned in the right place.

The rest of our time at the park was more of the same. Dion licked Dorito dust off his fingers, I fed Brianna small bites of sandwich, and Daddy played the perfect pretend father with Tina pretending to care about us by his side. He acted like nothing mattered, like he didn't owe us anything—and he didn't. He never apologized for abandoning us after the Tornado, never tried to explain, never admitted he'd messed up.

After all that chaos, my parents thought it was a great idea to ship Dion and me off to live with Daddy in Los Angeles, while Brianna stayed with Mom. But that didn't work out.

Then he started attending Set Free Church—the place that ruined our chances of ever getting our father back. A place full of ex-bikers, ex-drug addicts, ex-gang members. The Men lived at The House of Paul, the women at The House of Ruth, including Tina, who was also the pastor's niece. She sang in the choir; Dad joined, and poof, suddenly this was all our new reality.

Now, sitting in this little park, next to him, I was expecting— hoping even—for a real apology. At least some form of grown-up explanation. Something to acknowledge what he'd done. But no, nothing was offered.

As the sun began to set, I realized we'd leave without that conversation. And then he said the words that made my stomach drop:

"Guess what? You guys are coming to spend the night."

Latrice had been right. He *was* going to try to kidnap us. Not on my watch.

"Don't we need to ask Mom?" I said quickly.

"We already did," Tina said, gleefully.

"I wasn't talking to you," I snapped.

Dad jumped in. "Mommy packed your stuff while we were here so we could take you back to Anaheim with us. You ready?"

I picked up Brianna, kept my cool, and walked toward the car. Dion shouted, "Yeah!" I just followed behind, both worried and confused.

When we got home, Tina waited behind again. My mother took me into the bathroom and shut the door.

"Your toothbrushes are at the bottom of the bag. Be good and don't let your brother and sister out of your sight for one second."

"I won't."

"Okay, gimmie' a kiss." I kissed my mother on the cheek, then I reared my head back to look in her eyes.

She asked me with her head tilted to the side. "Did you like Tina?"

"No."

"Well, alright." My mom didn't show any emotion. She only pursed he lips and raised her eyebrows.

On the way to his house, my dad put in a cassette tape of him singing with the Set Free Choir. He told us about how they were going to Egypt and the Middle East, traveling to distant places to perform on stage and glorify God, and a bizarre story about how the blood of Jesus had saved them.

All this religious talk made Tina light up. She wouldn't stop talking about God, Jesus, and the Holy Spirit. She didn't have enough sense to know you needed a spoon to eat pudding, but she knew all about the rapture and the mark of the beast.

That car ride over felt like forever. I started wishing this rapture would hurry up and happen right now, so I wouldn't have to hear her annoying pothead voice about it all anymore.

I couldn't have cared less whether or not Jesus had forgiven my dad. I was still waiting for my apology because I'm not Jesus, and I hadn't forgiven him.

When we arrived, I wasn't ready for the large group of people who flooded out of that house like roaches, and by the looks of it, I knew the place had to be crawling with the real kind too.

I wondered if it was someone's birthday party because all these little kids came running up to my dad, screaming, "Paul, Paul, Paul!"

My dad turned to me and said, "This is Matthew, he's your same-age son." And this is Phillip and Trina. They're Pastor Phil's kids. Since I had no idea, on earth, who pastor Phil was, I couldn't have cared less.

Matthew, the oldest, came over to me, and since he was cute, I was nice to him. This Matthew person got to see my daddy every day, while my siblings and I were thirty-two infinite miles apart from him.

Wondering every day if he was okay or if he was back in jail again. When we ate dinner, I hoped he was eating something too.

What was he eating? I worried about where he slept and if he had blankets and pillows to keep him warm and comfortable.

Most nights, I spent visualizing his face, His happy face with his big, gleaming smile. Hoping he wasn't dead or beaten up somewhere. Other times, I'd lie in bed, tearing up, feeling like it had been a lifetime since he last sang to us until we fell asleep.

We walked down the left side of the house, paved in asphalt, which surprised me. It felt more like the parking lot of a business or a school playground to me.

People's big, weird eyes, coffee-stained teeth, and mustaches followed us as they oohed and awed, saying things like, "They look just like you, Paul," and "Oh, they're so pretty!"

The backyard was lined with picnic tables and folding chairs along a chain-link fence that backed up to an alley.

We rounded the house and climbed onto an enclosed back porch with a washer and dryer, just before the kitchen door. The smell hit me first: musty wood, farts, and Spanish-style rice. There were people in every corner. Still no cake. No balloons. No streamers.

What the hell are all these people doing here?

Finally, I asked, "Is it someone's birthday?"

"No son."

"Then why are there so many people here?"

"They live here."

I almost fell over.

"All of them?"

"The ladies live at The House of Ruth, next door, but the men live here."

Still disbelief: "All of them?" I asked again.

"Yes, son, all of 'em."

We walked through the kitchen into what was supposed to be a dining room, though it was mostly a lounging area. A small bathroom sat off to the side near the stairs.

As we passed it, damp air rolled out like an unhappy ghost. My dad led us upstairs, but the smell of mold under Irish Spring made me peek into the shower.

It was a disaster: black grout, missing tiles, a stiff curtain that looked like it might walk off on its own. I didn't know whether to feel worse for him or me since I'd have to eventually endure bathing in there.

At the top of the stairs was one large room filled with bunk beds. In the center, under the slanted ceiling, sat a full-size bed. Sleeping bags, storage bins, suitcases, lamps, and books lined the walls. Clothes hung from ceiling beams on mismatched hangers. Every bed was made tight, Navy-style.

I didn't have to ask. This was everybody's room—and now it was ours too, for the night.

Dad slid our bags under the full-size bed.

"You guys wanna go outside and play?"

Dion shouted, "Yeah!" and ran downstairs. Normally, I would've told him not to run, but today I was off duty. Let Daddy be the other parent for a change.

I tried to sneak out the front, but that porch turned out to be more sleeping space. So I doubled back through the kitchen—right into Tina at the stove in an apron, stirring something that smelled exactly like the house.

"I hope you guys like Mexican food."

"We do, but we won't like what you're making,"

"Oh no? Well, that's what's for dinner.

I thought, *Girl, please, that's what's for your dinner.*

When my dad caught up with me, I tilted my head, walked slowly over, and put my arms around his waist, looking up with my best puppy-dog eyes.

"Daddy, Dion and Brianna won't like that food. Can we go to Jack in the Box instead, please?"

That's what you call pulling out the big guns. He didn't hesitate.

"We'll be back!" He said to Rosarita over there at the stove. Just like that, we escaped around the corner. Finally, we had Daddy all to ourselves.

Outside, he carried Dion. I held Brianna. Inside Jack in the Box, the cold air hit us like heaven.

He flirted with the cashier. I rolled my eyes. We ordered burgers, fries, and milkshakes and sat down together—just the four of us.

I patiently waited for the talk. The apology. Something. Anything.

No one else was there to make him feel small or make him feel stupid about what he would say. No condescending Dianna, no "Miss New Bootie" to impress.

It didn't even matter what he said about why things were so mixed up, as long as he said something, anything to erase it from the normal category and place it into the—this shouldn't have happened category.

But instead of teaching us the importance of apologizing for bad behavior, he only sang, joked, kissed our ears, and did his best to make us laugh as if laughter was the key to forgetting.

By the time we finished eating and headed back, it was dark, so it was bedtime, but even worse than that, it was going to be, you guessed it, shower time.

"Daddy, you guys have bleach…right?"

# LET ME TELL YOU SOMETHIN

*O*nce we were out of the car, Tina popped up out of nowhere like a shapeshifter from another dimension.

"Did you have fun?" She kept asking me questions as if I'd given her some reason to think I liked her.

"It's time for us to take a shower," I said, not looking at her.

"I'll take Brianna over to my place and give her a bath in the tub."

"No! My mother told me not to let her out of my sight."

"It's okay, Paulie," my dad said, trying to soften it.

"Then I'm going to call my mom."

"But there's no tub here, and there's no phone," Tina said, as if she'd won.

"I saw a payphone across the street at Guadalajara's Restaurant. I know how to call collect."

My dad stepped in. "We'll wash her in the sink. How about that?"

That was fine. I wasn't letting some woman Brianna had never met take her off to a place called The House of Ruth, full of strangers. Not on my watch.

After Brianna was clean and in her nightgown, I tried to get Dion into the shower. He refused. For once, I didn't care. I washed myself fast, careful not to let the funk of the place get on me.

Heading upstairs, I heard someone say, "Pssst."

There she was again—Tina—beckoning me from the kitchen.

"Come here. I have a surprise."

I followed her to the oval wooden table and sat in the chair facing the kitchen so I could see what she was bringing and prepare my reaction.

On the wall was a crooked paint-by-numbers picture of an old man praying over bread and a bowl. He looked like he was thinking the same thing I was: *Where am I, and what is this place?*

Tina came back holding a plate stacked with lemon cookies and a big glass of milk, a paper towel fluttering between her fingers.

"Ta-da."

Before she could set them down, I folded my hands on the table.

"What do you say?" she asked, as if I should feel obliged to thank her.

The silence stretched between us.

"We don't eat store-bought baked goods," I said. "And we don't drink milk. It's for baby cows."

Her face changed. Just like that.

I cleared my throat. "My mom bakes for us."

"Well, I guess I'll give these to the other kids," she said.

"Okay. Goodnight."

"Wait," she said. "How long have your mom and dad been divorced?"

"You should ask my dad. He's your boyfriend, isn't he?"

"He said they fought a lot. Did he ever hit her?"

I just looked at her.

"Don't worry," I said. "Everything you think he did to her will happen to you, too. Only worse."

"That wasn't nice."

"That's okay," I said assuredly. "Let me tell you something, you're nobody to me, and I don't have to be nice to you."

I left her sitting there, finally exposed—no fake smiles, no innocent act—from either of us.

Upstairs, Dion and Brianna were curled up beside my dad. I slid in on the other side, tucked myself under his arm the way we used to.

The calming hum of the box fans made it easier for me to examine my dad in peace.

It had been so long since I'd seen him. I figured I'd better hurry up if I wanted to absorb enough of the memory of him to last me another long while.

With my head on his chest, I listened to the air filling his lungs, then the long stream of release going out. I tried to match his breathing with mine so that my chest rose at the same time.

Staring at his face, I wondered whether or not I would grow hair on my face one day, too. Lightly tracing his moustache with my index finger, I thought to myself, "How does hair even grow out of your face, and does it hurt?" I made mental pictures of his nose, his eyebrows, his ears, and his lips.

Then I examined the lines on his forehead, and the way it looked sort of mean and Frankenstein-like. I remembered Frankenstein wasn't mean after all, but rather mistreated instead. I didn't even know yet that Frankenstein wasn't even the monster's name.

He had put on some weight, so his muscles were back and bigger than ever. I wanted to have muscles like that one day.

I wanted to have all the things I thought made my daddy handsome, the things that made him look strong on the outside, too.

Then there was the opposite; I also knew that I wanted none

of the things that allowed him to live casually, while knowing that every day without him there, I was grappling with being a little boy who could only imagine what it was like to have a father at home.

A real-life father there to protect him, to correct him, to love him. Cut his steak, tie his shoe, tell him "Just shake it off, man."

*Wouldn't that be nice, huh? Think about it. To be one of those little boys who could lie there together with their dad, looking up at the ceiling or maybe sometimes outside, flat-backed, side by side on the grass, gazing into the day or the night sky.*

*Or not even looking at all. Maybe with both their eyes closed while trying to match one another's breath, seeing who can hold it in, or who can blow it out the longest.*

*Then, we or they, this imaginary father and son in my mind, would make fun of each other for lying about how many seconds they held their breath for.*

*Maybe they'd play basketball or football or something—together. And even if the little boy wasn't good at it, the dad would always keep teaching him, and neither the dad nor the little boy would ever get tired of playing for hours and hours.*

*Perhaps the dad would put his arm around the son's neck when they were both laughing at something silly or stupid. Sometimes he'd give him a smack on the cheek and tell him, "Good job, son," for something cool he'd done.*

*Most of all, when they were playing a game like chess or checkers or even Go Fish, he would never just let the little boy win easily, either.*

*That way, when he really did win, he would know the true feeling of being a real winner. The boy would know that feeling forever, and all because of his dad, who made him feel like he meant everything.*

# GETTING A GRIP

When we got back from our visit with Daddy, something about my mother felt off. She was a bit distant, and her attention seemed to be focused elsewhere. Instead of telling us what to do, she was simply letting things happen. We could even eat cereal on weekdays without having to beg for it.

Her pager buzzed and beeped more than usual with codes like 07734 *hello*, 823 *thinking of you*, and 143 for *I love you*. When 69 started showing up on the screen, my little grown ass definitely knew something was up. I learned all about that one during recess at school.

She stayed on the phone longer, but I didn't say anything. At least there was no fighting. No shouting. No static crackling through the walls. What if she found a nice, handsome man who loved her? I thought that would be great.

My fingernails had started growing back. The bleeding hang-nails from me biting them had stopped. The ache in my stomach during school went quiet. I stopped worrying about coming home to find one parent dead at the hands of the other. The lies about handprints on my face had faded, and my lips healed now that I wasn't licking them raw from nerves.

Life felt lighter. Carefree, even. I floated through it cautiously, enjoying the calm in measured doses. As long as I remembered it could all end at any moment, I wouldn't shatter when it did.

We played outside until we were called in. Our little family, the four of us, cuddled on the sofa to watch movies or play games together. Dianna was figuring out her true normal for us, and our normal was good enough for me, so I started to like this new apartment, these new kids around us, and even my new school.

My new fourth-grade teacher, Mrs. Cooks, was a big lady—tall like a man, with wide feet, thick ankles, and great-big hands. I'm sure most women wouldn't take that as a compliment, but I meant it as one. To me, those things felt like safety.

They told me she could kick some ass if the moment called for it. And then there was her voice—soprano, soft, verging on elegant—floating out of a body that looked like it could stop trouble before it ever got started.

She took no nonsense, but she was kind with it. The kind of teacher who could shut a room down and still make you feel seen. Our classroom was carpeted in that ugly orange-and-brown short pile, and when she walked, her shoes dragged softly against it, a steady sound that always let you know when she was coming.

I started at Arroyo Elementary late in the fourth grade, so Mrs. Cooks placed my desk right beside hers to help me settle in—or at least that's how I understood it.

Since my cursive was neat and careful, she let me write the lesson plans on the chalkboard, pass out papers when they were needed, and at the end of the day, clean the erasers by banging them against a wet rag outside.

The school was a little rough, sure—but nowhere near as bad as the one we'd left behind in Los Angeles.

One day, while we were standing in line to head out to lunch, a little girl named Stephanie got it into her mind that I needed to pay attention to her. From behind me, she shouted, "Look at me!"

"What do you want?" I said without turning around.

"I said, look at me!"

Man, she was an ugly-looking little girl, too. Known for her loud mouth, runny nose, and her braids that needed to be taken down and redone.

Mrs. Cooks with eyes and ears all over said, "Stephanie, shut your mouth up girl, and leave that boy alone."

As our teacher walked ahead of us to get the line moving, that horrible little bitch Stephanie slapped me hard in the back of the head. What she didn't know was that I'd already been hit in the head more times than I could count. It didn't faze me—but it was about to faze her.

In an instant, a strange heat flooded my body, rising fast and settling heavy in my forehead, pulsing between my eyes. My shoulders locked up, tight and ready, like something inside me had been flipped on. I felt it clearly then: if I didn't defend myself, I would freeze. I would be stuck there forever.

So I didn't freeze.

In one swift motion, I turned and started slapping her head with everything I had. I didn't stop when she fell either. I grabbed onto her braids, using them to keep her still, and kept hitting her. I didn't know the word for it yet, but the rage was already living in me.

We didn't call it PTSD back then, but this was my first real introduction to the way violence—any violence—could pull something feral and unstoppable straight out of me.

I screamed at her, "There—now everybody's looking at you! See? See? See?"

I kept yelling it, over and over: "Don't you ever touch me again! Don't you ever touch me again!"

Mrs. Cooks let me get it out a few more times before she

finally moved in to pull me off her. When she pried what was left of those braids from my hands, she already knew who had started it.

Once we were separated, Stephanie was sent to the office, and I was told to go back into the classroom.

"Sit right here and wait for me."

"I will."

I wanted to cry, but I was still too angry. The sadness came from somewhere deeper—the realization that I had disappointed my teacher. That was the part that hurt the most. This woman, who had made me her favorite, was going to cast me out now. Suspension didn't even matter. I was sure I was out of her good graces now, forever.

With that thought settling in, I folded my arms on the desk, laid my head down, and cried. After a few minutes, and after thinking *that's what stupid Stephanie gets*, I pulled myself back together.

When the classroom door opened again, it was our principal, Mrs. Erby. I had never—not once—been in trouble with the principal before, but I knew who she was. Mrs. Erby had been one of my aunt's favorite teachers, which somehow made this feel even more serious.

"You're Dianna DiOssi's son?" she asked.

"Yes, Mrs. Erby," I said, wiping tears from my cheeks.

"Betty DiOssi's grandson?"

"Yes."

"And Gina DiOssi is your aunt—is that right?"

"Yes."

"I was your aunt's teacher when she was in school," she said. "She was one of my favorites."

"Yes, ma'am. She's my favorite aunt."

By then, Mrs. Cooks had returned and was seated quietly at her desk.

Mrs. Erby went on, "Stephanie is being suspended for hitting you in the back of the head for no reason."

"Okay," I said, unsure what I was allowed to feel yet.

"Stephanie comes from a family of troublemakers," she added. "I had her mother as a student, too."

Mrs. Cooks turned toward me, laughing, and said, "Paul, these little funky kids at this school are gonna be jealous of you for a lotta things, and don't you forget it. But after the way you knocked ol' Stephanie around, they not gon' try you again, that's fa sho'."

I had never heard my teacher talk like that before, and it made me laugh—even though I still didn't know whether I was officially in the clear for fighting.

Then she reached into her little mini fridge and pulled out a container of cottage cheese, a plastic spoon, and an Abba-Zabba.

"I like my Abba-Zabba's cold," she said. "Makes 'em last longer. Here—have it. It'll make you feel better."

I was still young enough to think teachers couldn't know certain things, so it struck me as oddly funny to hear Mrs. Cooks say "Abba-Zabba"—and even stranger that she knew the trick about putting them in the fridge.

Mrs. Erby's voice cut through my amusement.

"I have to call your mother and tell her what happened, understand?"

"Yes, Mrs. Erby. How long am I suspended for?"

She flashed a devil-may-care smile. "You are not suspended, young man."

Oh, the relief!

"You did something that all of us wanted to do," she continued. "I'll have them bring you a lunch tray from the cafeteria. And listen to me—don't you ever let these kids push you around. Got that?"

That encouragement carried me through the rest of elementary school, and I owe those two women for it—because being a kid in the '80s was just fucking hard. When Stephanie eventually came back to school, she still had her big mouth, but she kept it shut around me. In the classroom, she avoided my eyes, and on the playground, she stayed away like there was a court order with my name on it.

That year, no one put their hands on me again. It was still iffy —I was always banking on not getting in trouble with my mother for fighting—but no one tried me.

My mother may have beaten me herself, at times, for no reason, and she may have traumatized me into believing she would kill me if I disobeyed her, but I will give her this: she never raised me to be a victim of the outside world.

This was the best advice she ever gave me:

"If somebody puts their hands on you, I want you to beat them like you're tryin' to kill 'em."

And that wasn't all…

"I don't care if you have to pick up something and beat them to death. Do not let anybody get away with putting their hands on you."

She meant it. It was harsh, sure—but the world we were living in demanded it.

When school let out that day, I went to find Dion so we could walk home together. Lost in my own thoughts, I worried I was overdue for a whoppin after going so long without one. When we reached the front door, the security screen was shut, but the door itself was wide open, the television already on.

My mom was home.

And I knew I was in for it.

When we got inside, Dion and I called out, "Hi, Mommy!"

"How was school?" she asked.

"Good!" we sang in unison. I couldn't speak for Dion, but I knew my little ass was lying.

"Mrs. Erby called me at work about that fight you had with that girl," she said. "Did she hit you first?"

"Yes," I answered, steady and prepared for whatever was coming next.

"Good," she said. "Then I'm glad you tore her little ass up." Then, just like that: "Let's order some pizza for dinner."

All three of us—Brianna included—floated straight up onto cloud nine.

"So what happened?" she asked, her tone more Latrice than Mommy. For the first time, I saw her not as someone I had to brace myself against, but as someone I could trust. Maybe it was my age fooling me, or maybe she was starting to see that I was growing up. Either way, I was there for it, and I liked it.

I told her everything, from start to finish. She especially enjoyed the part where I wrapped my hand into Stephanie's braids so I could get a good grip.

# ACTIVATOR

While growing up, my mother had been severely bullied for having a "white daddy." Her mother told her never to fight back. Little girls were never supposed to fight.

She was told to scream and run away to get a teacher. That, she was told, was the only proper way to handle a bully.

Of course, my grandmother later denied ever saying it. Since my mother didn't beat me for fighting, I knew now, for certain, that defending myself was one of the things that mattered most to her.

It was hard to settle into the comfort of not being smacked around for such a long time. These days, my mother looked more like the happy her that I had always longed to see.

Her happy look reminded me of where I got my happy look from. When we smiled, we looked like twins—our lips the same shape, our teeth too, except hers were a bit crooked.

Many times she told me, "When I was pregnant, I prayed that God would give you beautiful, straight teeth—and he did."

I was starting to think that maybe we could do just fine on our own, and that with Daddy out of the picture, my mother could discover who she was supposed to be—for herself and for all of us.

As the days went by, my mother started talking on the phone for long hours. Her pager was blowing up, left and right.

The way she spoke to whoever was on the other end made her sound like a teenager straight out of one of those bad '80s movies. She twirled the cord around her finger and whispered things whenever I walked by.

She even started taking the phone into her room and shutting the door. Soon after, the mood shifted back to a "speak only when spoken to" regime, just like before—the way it had been when she sat at home on Chanslor Street, piping hot mad because Daddy was out somewhere smoking, snorting, or fucking something he shouldn't have been.

Then it happened. The other foot dropped, and it landed right on my neck, where it stayed between us for a long while.

One day, after she got home from work, we were sitting at the dinner table, eating the cube steak with ketchup that I had seasoned and "started" for her in the broiler, the veg-all with a dash of Lawry's, and the white rice with butter and salt.

That's when she just blurted out, "Doug is moving in with us to help pay the rent."

"Who is Doug?" I asked in a haze of confusion.

"Valentina's brother Doug."

"Valentina's brother Doug?"

"Yeah, Phillips' Uncle. You remember him."

"The one with the Jerry Curl, who falls asleep on his motor-cycle all the time?"

"No, the other one."

"The really tall one with the Jerry Curl?"

"No, he's the really buff one, with the muscles and the Jerry Curl."

*Why couldn't there be at least one without a damn Jerry Curl? We had just gotten this brand-new sofa. Now the back cushions were gonna get ruined for sure. Activator juice everywhere!*

"Oh, the one from the motel that time?" I asked. She had met up with him before.

"Why is he coming to live with us, Mommy? Doesn't he already have a place to live?"

Get this—she told me it was because they loved each other. Not just because he could help pay the rent. They loved each other...imagine that. Now, how the fuck?

Love, huh? As if either of them had the faintest idea what love even was. At least, that's what she wanted me to believe—that somehow, with her history in relationships and all the "wisdom" she carried, they were going to show the world what love looked like. Please.

Soon enough, I blinked, and he was moved in. Doug, with a black duffel bag full of who-knows-what drugs and trash bags stuffed with swap-meet clothes. It was November, and his birthday was coming up, so everything became about him—and, of course, his kids had to be there too.

My mother encouraged Brianna to call him "Daddy" right away. Dion, on the other hand, hid like a bunny from a coyote. Me? I stayed flippant, treating Doug like an annoying, overstayed houseguest— I hated him. Hated the way he looked, like one of the crows from *The Wiz*, hated the way he talked, hated that he thought he was important.

One day, after emerging from the bedroom together, Doug and Mom sat me down at the table. They had created a "chore chart" on a paper plate and stuck it to the fridge with a magnet. Brilliant plan, right? A way for him not to lift a finger while I became the servant of the house.

Overnight, my life transformed into one long list of mandatory duties: keeping the house spotless, helping my siblings with homework, you name it, it was my job.

I cleaned the cracks and crevices, mopped floors until they squeaked, ironed clothes, thawed meat, tucked my siblings in, folded laundry, dusted furniture, brought things from one room to another, handwashed and rehung drapes. I scrubbed the stovetop with steel wool until my fingers were pruned and my nails were all scratched up.

I went months without a haircut while Doug got his Jerry Curl done on schedule. And I did it all silently, without asking why or using the word "but."

It worked out perfectly for them because it left them free to fuck. Fuck, fuck, fuck. Loudly. Constantly. So loud that I became obsessed with protecting my siblings' ears from the sound.

Every day, I devised a new game, a new distraction.

"Let's go outside, let's watch TV in the living room with the door shut."

Anything to preserve their innocence, since mine was already shot to shit.

But innocence is fragile. And ours was getting shredded to bits. I was learning things far too early—what sex could sound like, what it could look like, what it could ultimately mean.

And let me tell you, I've had some amazing sex in my life, but none of it would have been worth letting my children hear it with some man who wasn't even their own father.

I didn't know much about Doug except this: he knew how to fuck, and he had no shame doing it while my siblings and I were within earshot. Disgusted, I finally said something to Mom, trying to be respectful:

"Mommy, sometimes we can hear you and Doug in the room."

"That's none of your business," she said… End of conversation.

Doug wins again. Doug, the drug dealer. Doug, the ex-convict. Doug, the cheat, the drug user. He was the reason the police raided our apartment at gunpoint, the reason I found cocaine in a duffel bag in Mom's closet. Doug, the man who watched me shower, the man who turned on the Playboy channel and pretended to sleep while his penis pointed straight out of his boxers. Doug, the man who asked me if I had hair down there yet. The man who destroyed our Christmas ornaments and traumatized my family.

Doug wasn't just a person in our house—he was an evil force. The manifestation of an illness, one, we had no choice but to survive.

My mother was suffering from Dickmatization. Yes, an invented word, because what else could you call it? That tragic condition in which otherwise competent, intelligent people lose all sense of reason for a man who's… well, let's just say he's very accomplished in the bedroom. Motherly duties? Forgotten. Priorities? Shattered. Minds? Entirely occupied by one thing and one thing only: that dangerously good dick.

We've all seen it. Maybe even lived it. Friends, aunts, cousins, mothers—suddenly reduced to nothing more than human magnets for bad decisions. And don't you dare bring evidence to the contrary. No proof, no logic, no facts can sway a Dickmatized person. You could have a court summons and a signed confession, and they'd still glare at you like you were the enemy.

If there were a pharmaceutical cure for this, it would be called Gowitout. Take one dose, and suddenly, priorities return. Household chores get done. Children get fed on time, and if it doesn't work, at least you have a funny commercial in your head: "Do you or a loved one suffer from Dickmatization? Ask your oldest son— he'll tell you."

Now, let me be clear: I'm not just mocking. This is real. I grew up with it. I watched it happen. I saw how love—or sex masqueraded as such—could turn the smartest, most capable person into a hostage of lust. And yet… there's something deeply human about it. It's absurd, ridiculous, and infuriating, yes, but also painfully, undeniably part of life. The humor shields the chaos—the dignity is found through surviving it.

In the end, I understood that my mother had taught me how to fight back, even as she was losing a different battle herself—and that contradiction would shape everything that came next.

# NOTHING WILL HAPPEN

The glittering desert city of Las Vegas is three hundred forty-five miles from Pomona. If you stopped for gas just once and drove straight through, it took three hours and fifty-six minutes by car.

A bus could get you there in about six hours and fifty-one minutes, with limited pit stops for food, bathroom breaks, stretching your legs, and such. Taking a red-eye out of Ontario Airport got you there in only an hour and seventeen minutes.

And if you had to walk—as if it were your life's ambition to land in the Guinness Book—it could be done in ninety hours. Just about four days.

One Friday night, after being plied with Pizza, potato chips, candy bars, and lemonade—after being told we could stay up as late as we wanted as long as we agreed not to answer the phone or open the front door—my siblings and I were left completely alone so that Dianna and her boyfriend could drive to Sin City in the middle of the night.

Of course, I wasn't told where they were going or any of the details. I wouldn't learn the truth until after they returned. I had been bamboozled by the only person on Earth capable of bamboozling me.

Dianna.

As she kissed us on the cheek, one by one, she said, "We'll be back really late, so if you get sleepy, just go to bed."

"But Mom, where are you going?"

"That's none of your business. Do not open the living room curtains, and don't answer the door or the phone. Let the answering machine pick up—but if it's me, you answer it. You hear me?"

"Yes."

I agreed under duress, already knotted with anxiety about the unknown stretch of time she was leaving us alone. I was terrified of making the wrong decision if something happened to Dion or Brianna.

If I wasn't allowed to use the phone or open the door, how was I supposed to protect them? What if someone broke through the window, and I needed to call the police?

Since Doug started keeping the guns in the trunk of his car instead of my mother's closet, the big knife in the kitchen drawer would have to be my only protection.

"Yes, what?" Doug chimed in.

"Yes… Ma'am," I said, dragging out the words to underline my disdain for this new "slavery" vernacular. We weren't southerners. Never had been. But his family was, and if he liked it, Mom loved it, so I had to play along.

"Can I call Mom-Mom if anything happens?"

"No, nothing is going to happen. Do not touch that phone, do you understand?"

"Yes." I couldn't win, so I stopped asking.

"Yes, what?" the high school dropout and drug dealer pressed.

I fixed him with a look and said, "Don't you mean… yes, who?"

My mother grabbed her purse, and out the door they went.

She locked the deadbolt, then the security screen. I could hear their voices fading, the car doors shutting, the engine starting—and then nothing. Silence.

We had two big pizzas, a two-liter of lemonade, a giant bag of sour cream and onion Ruffles, Snickers, Dots, Junior Mints, and Abba Zababs. Any other little boy would've thought they'd died and gone to heaven. Another kid might've figured out a way to sneak his friends in and watch dirty movies on Skin-a-max.

Me? I was only worried about the safety of the two other little people left under my charge. I couldn't believe it. I was in denial. You know how sometimes you hear other kids wish they were grown-ups? Well, I never did.

This all had to be some kind of test—to see if I'd peek through the curtains or try the door, or do something I wasn't supposed to do. Maybe she wanted to see if I'd call my grandmother and tell her we were home alone.

I started convincing myself that she'd only gone around the corner to the 7-Eleven, where she'd wait a while and then call to check on us. I imagined the phone ringing until the answering machine picked up, and her smiling voice saying, *"Gotcha. It was just a test. You did well, son."*

*"Oh, how I love you. You're such a good boy—and I kicked Doug's ass out, too."*

We sat there quietly, watching *Willow* on HBO for the one-millionth time, when the phone finally rang. I jumped up and ran to the kitchen. Then I hesitated—maybe I should have gone to Mom's room instead.

One hand held my ham-and-pineapple slice, the other hovered over the receiver. I let the phone ring... and ring... and ring, expecting the machine to pick up at any moment. But it didn't. By the ninth ring, I answered.

"DiOssi residence," I said, hoping she'd like that.

"Is yo mama gone yet?"

"Doug?" My stomach sank—of all people, it had to be him.

"No, boy, it's JB. They gone yet?"

"No, they're still here," I feigned, my voice tight with fear. Doug's younger brother was just as untrustworthy.

"No, dey ain't," he said, as if he knew better than I did.

I slammed the phone down and immediately regretted answering it at all. Less than ten seconds passed before it started ringing again.

*Maybe this time it's her.*

*Maybe I shouldn't answer.*

*If this is just a test, she'll be back soon. Everything will be fine.*

I tried to reason with myself—sit back down, eat the pizza, stop worrying. Just turn the ringer off. You don't have to answer it.

"Hello," I said anyway.

"You remember Lance, right?"

"Stop calling here, JB!"

"We gon' come over there and fuck you in the ass, you little faggot."

"Yeah, we gon' fuck your little faggot ass—Haaa haa!" His friend Lance yelled in the background. He was a cholo who grew up on the same street as Doug's family.

I slammed the phone back into its cradle and ran—straight for the hallway closet. I grabbed one of the extra bed sheets and hurried to the kitchen window, covering the gap between the valance and the bottom of the curtains. If they came to the apartment, at least they wouldn't be able to see inside. At least we could hide a little better.

After that, I went into my mom's room and wedged the stick into the base of the sliding glass door. I tightened the bolt at the top, just in case. The bars on our bedroom window gave me a small sense of relief—some kind of barrier, however flimsy.

I started planning. I could move the food into our bedroom

and turn on the little TV in there. I could shut the hallway door and drag one of my mom's nightstands in front of it.

Then I could close our bedroom door and push the dresser in front of that, too. If we had to use the bathroom, I would just push it back out of the way. I would take the big knife and hide it between my mattress and the box spring so that Dion and Brianna wouldn't see it.

That way we'd be safe. Everything would be okay. *We're okay... We're okay.*

I yelled out with phony excitement, "Come on, you guys, let's take the food into our room!"

I checked the front door to make sure it was locked. Eating in the room was normally a big no-no, but to Dion, it just sounded like fun. Brianna, as usual, wanted to do whatever we were doing, so we all headed toward the room without any fuss about the TV in there being smaller.

"Grab all the candy, I'll get the rest," I said.

I moved quickly, faking calm while doing my best to hide the frantic shaking of my hands as I quietly swiped the big knife from the kitchen.

The fierceness in my eyes had to be held in check, too. I couldn't let them see my fear—if they did, they'd be scared too. I kept repeating in my mind.

*Just get them in the room. Please, just get them in the room,*

We settled into our little haven, but only just—for now. Dion and Brianna weren't bickering over their usual things, like who got more potato chips or whose slice of pizza was bigger. *Willow* had ended, and now *Howard the Duck* was on, but time crawled.

I wished we could fall asleep, wake up tomorrow, and have all of this just be over.

When I noticed the sky darkening outside, I went to turn off the lights in the kitchen and living room. It had to look like no one was home. Maybe I could fool JB into thinking someone had come to get us.

Even though I'd already checked, my OCD made me double-check the front door one last time.

*Locked. Good.*

Walking from the kitchen, across the living room, I heard a man's voice. I thought, "Maybe it's Ross, the neighbor." Anything to convince my fears to go away. Then I heard a second man's voice. It was Lance and JB for sure.

I knew their voices, alright. It seemed like any time we were at Doug's mother's house playing with the other kids in the backyard, the two of them were always there, teasing us or saying something dirty or mean.

One of their older girl cousins, a girl named Adrianne, with lots of pimples, told me that Lance took her virginity, but she said it was okay because she asked him to.

Frozen in place, I heard tap, tap, tap, on the screen door.

"Aye, Paulie, open up the door, lil man!" JB said in the most casual of voices imaginable.

As if he were my favorite uncle, or an old friend. This fool acted like he never said what he said to me over the phone. Maybe he just wanted me to think that what he had done was normal behavior, like I was an idiot.

The adults around me were constantly underestimating my intelligence, and I was getting sick and tired of it—especially when it came from stupid Doug's even more stupid brother.

What the fuck was wrong with these people, anyway?

Why would he do this to a scared kid who was just minding his own business? And why did everything, when it came to me, have to be about sex with these disgusting-ass grown men?

I couldn't fucking blink without some man trying to pull me one step closer to his dick.

Calmly leaning my back against the wall between the door and the window—careful not to touch the curtains—I cleared my throat before wildly shouting at the top of my lungs, "I'm calling 911 right now! I'm calling 911! I'm calling 911!"

I said it a few times, just to make sure the idiot on the other side of the door didn't misunderstand me. I acted it all out, word for word.

"Hello, please send the police. I'm only ten years old, and we're home alone. There are two strangers outside our door who look like gang members. One is Black and one is Mexican, and I think they have a gun. Please hurry—I think they want to kill us. Our address is 1388 Murchison Avenue, apartment number two."

By the time I got to the address, in my phony, ad-libbed cry for help, I heard the screech of tires. That sound told me everything I needed to know—we were safe from whatever JB had planned.

Now all I had to do was tell Mom-Mom.

# 947-8340

’d had enough. All of it. And no matter what my mother said, the next move had to be a call to my grandmother.

My fingers dialed like crazy. Nine. Four. Seven. Eight. Three. Four. Zero.

"DiOssi residence," she answered, a smile in her voice.

"Hi, Mom-Mom. It's Paulie." My voice cracked as I cried just a little.

"Hi, buttons. Are you crying? What's wrong?"

How could I tell her? How could I explain what was happening —what he'd said—without actually saying it?

"Mom and Doug left us here a long time ago," I said. "She told me she'd be gone all night. Then JB called the house and said some nasty, grown-up sex things to me. Then he tried to come over with Lance. I'm scared."

"Is he there now?" Her voice sharpened.

"No. I pretended to call the police while they were outside."

"Is the door locked?"

"Yes."

"Don't open it. Don't open it for anyone. We're on our way."

I hung up and ran into the bedroom. Dion and Brianna looked up at me.

Mustering up a fake smile, I threw my hands in the air and announced, "We're spending the night at Mom-Mom and Pop-Pop's tonight!"

"Yay!"

"Woo-hoo!"

That was all the explanation they needed.

I moved like a blur. Gathering toothbrushes, pajamas. Brianna's nightgown and hair supplies. Shoes. Clothes for the next day. I stuffed everything into a pillowcase.

Then I went back to the kitchen and returned the big knife from under my mattress to the drawer where it belonged.

Sooner than I expected, I heard my grandmother's voice on the other side of the front door.

"Paulie, it's us. Open up. It's Mom-Mom and Pop-Pop."

I grabbed the deadbolt key from the wall, dropped it, fumbled with it, and finally got the door open.

My grandmother stood there with that familiar, tight expression—her face under pressure. My grandfather stood beside her in silence, holding his shotgun with the scope on it, one hand on the revolver tucked into his waistband.

On any given day, he already thought of himself as John Wayne. This was his moment.

Wrangler jeans. A massive belt buckle. Flannel shirt. Cowboy boots. An off-white cowboy hat with a feather tucked into the band. Born and raised in Wilmington, Delaware. I will never understand his devotion to the American West, but having him there, armed up, was a relief.

"Where are the kids?" my grandmother asked.

*Wasn't I one of them? Why was I never one of the kids?*

As if on cue, Dion and Brianna came running out. Pop-Pop lowered his weapon and scooped them into hugs instead.

"Let's get your stuff," he said to me.

"I already did."

As I hoisted the pillowcase over my shoulder, we headed out the door,

Instead of relief, the ride to my grandparents' house filled me with anxiety.

I had memorized their address for emergencies—just in case I was ever kidnapped, or found by the police after some terrible incident. I knew I would be safe there. I repeated it silently the entire drive east on the 60 freeway.

*1607 East Fairfield Court. Apartment Number Two. Ontario, California. 91761.*

The drive couldn't have felt longer if it were a slow-motion scene in a movie. I was paranoid as hell. I felt like Harriet Tubman, smuggling my brother and sister to freedom or something.

That fear wasn't imagined. I knew that once my mother found out I had told on her—told her parents—I was dead meat.

But what choice did I have? Grown men had been circling me like wolves. We were locked inside that apartment like animals in a zoo, and I was responsible for keeping Dion and Brianna alive.

It was too much. Far too much for one little boy.

When we got to my grandparents' house, the first thing we did was eat. Salami and cheese sandwiches. Whenever Pop-Pop was around, food was involved. He was Italian. That explains everything.

As soon as we finished eating, he left to go on a planned deer hunt with his buddies. That left us alone with Mom-Mom, which was fine by me. I didn't want to hunt anything, and Dion was too little anyway.

Night came fast, and with it, a living-room campout. Blankets covered the floor, topped with all the pillows from the beds. We settled in with popcorn, candy, and iced tea, ready to watch *Rats: Night of Terror*—until the scene where a man gets eaten alive scared Dion so badly, we had to change the channel.

The next morning, we woke to the smell of scrapple and eggs. Cinnamon raisin toast, butter, jelly—and bacon. Of course, there was bacon.

We sat down to eat when the phone rang.

My grandmother glanced at me before answering. Her face went serious.

"DiOssi residence."

A pause.

"They're here. And they're staying here."

That was it. She hung up.

I knew it was my mother. I didn't know where she was calling from—home, Las Vegas, Timbuktu, the moon. It didn't matter.

We finished breakfast. We showered. We got dressed. Mom-Mom struggled with Brianna's hair, so I took over.

We were sitting in the spare room listening to *The Woman in Red* on the record player when the doorbell rang—followed by furious pounding.

"Stay in here," my grandmother said.

Then the shouting started.

"What are they doing over here, Mom?"

"Why were they left alone, Dianna?"

"They were fine!"

"They were not fine, or they wouldn't be here!"

Their voices grew louder as they climbed the stairs.

"Do you know you could go to jail for leaving them like that?"

"Oh, Mom, shut up!"

I stood in front of the bedroom door just as it flew open, slamming into the wall.

My mother stood there gripping the doorknob, staring at me

with disgust. She didn't look like herself—hungover, exhausted, or both—but the rage was unmistakable.

"Do you know JB tried to come over there after Paulie?"

"What are you talking about? After Paulie?" she snapped. "He was probably just looking for us."

That was it.

The moment she chose to deny—*to erase*—what a grown man had threatened to do to me while she was gone, something inside me snapped.

"We're not leaving!" I screamed. "We're staying here with Mom-Mom and Pop-Pop!"

*Pow!*

She slapped me square in the mouth, hard enough to split the inside of my lip.

My grandmother lunged in front of me, but my mother grabbed my arm and started dragging me down the hallway. I dug my heels into the carpet, scraped my palms along the walls, tried to hook a corner—anything.

"Dion! Brianna! Get out here now! We're leaving!"

I twisted from my knees onto my butt as she hauled me toward the living room. At the top of the stairs, I managed to stand.

Mom-Mom tried to block her.

Then, we lost our footing. The three of us went tumbling down together—sliding, thumping, crashing into the entryway.

Dion and Brianna came scrambling down behind us.

And just like that, we were sitting in the back of our 1977 Cadillac Coupe De Ville. They must have gone to make a drug deal the night before, then wound up getting high together.

The ride home was eerie—it felt wrong in a way that made me believe the worst was yet to come.

My mother didn't say a word to me. Not one. That alone told me something was coming. The silence between her and

Doug in the front seat was even worse—no arguing, no laughing, just the radio blasting at a volume that pressed into my skull.

Doug didn't look angry. That was the terrifying part.

Whenever he got upset, his face never tightened or darkened. His eyes lit up instead—bright, alert, almost pleased. Even then, I knew that this is what evil looks like right before it does something awful.

We turned onto our street, and instead of slowing down, the car sped up.

Doug didn't pull into the carport. He drove straight onto the strip of grass that ran along the fence behind the apartments and slammed the car to a stop.

As we started to get out, everything happened at once.

Doug grabbed my mother by the hair.

He dragged her across the seat like she weighed nothing, pulling her over the console and out the driver's side door. She hit the ground hard.

"Mommy!" Dion screamed.

Brianna started crying.

I yelled, "Stop!" but it didn't matter.

In broad daylight, Doug dragged my mother by her hair around the building, past open windows, past neighbors who could see and hear everything—and he didn't care. He was smiling. A wide, satisfied smile, like this was exactly what he'd been waiting for.

The three of us ran behind him. I grabbed at his free arm, pulling, clawing, screaming, but he shook me off with one violent jerk.

He was strong—*prison strong*. Thick, compact, built like a wrestler.

"Let go of my mom!"

He shoved me clear across the room.

I scrambled back up just in time to see him slam the bedroom door shut and lock it.

And then the sounds started.

The bed was slamming into the wall so hard that the apartment felt like it might tip over. My mother pleaded underneath his weight. His breath. His grunting.

"Okay, Doug, please—wait. Ow!. Okay, wait. Please. I'm sorry. I'm sorry. Please—ow!"

Then the sobbing.

That was when I made Dion and Brianna go outside to play.

Instead of running to the neighbors, I went to the kitchen and got the big knife.

From where I crouched against the wall, I could hear her struggling to keep her voice down so we wouldn't hear her crying underneath his animal noises.

I slid down into a squat, my back against the wall, the knife heavy in my hand.

I planned it.

When that door opened, I would plunge the blade straight into his groin. I wouldn't hesitate. I wanted him to feel unrelenting shock first—confusion—then pain so sharp it would steal the very breath of him. When he doubled over, I would make sure he saw my face. I wanted him to know exactly who did this to him and why.

I wouldn't stop there.

I would blind him. I would make sure he could never look at anyone again. And if he screamed, if he begged, if he cried, I would make him repeat her words back to me—*please, wait, I'm sorry*—until he respected what they truly meant.

I would end him slowly. Carefully. Completely.

Not because I was born cruel.

Because I had already learned how violence worked, and I knew this was the only language men like him understood.

Maybe I was a hunter like Pop-Pop after all.

It never occurred to me to call the police until I thought about calling my grandmother.

That realization alone told me how warped my thinking had become.

I left my post and went for the phone in the kitchen, but when I lifted the receiver, there was nothing—no dial tone. The bedroom phone must have been off the hook. I didn't waste time fixing it. I ran.

Out the front door, down the alley, through the dirt field, straight to the 7-Eleven.

Eugene was behind the counter like always. The fluorescent lights hummed. Everything smelled like burnt coffee and floor cleaner.

"Can I use the phone, please?" I asked, already halfway around the counter.

He nodded.

Telling my grandmother that Doug was beating my mother took forever. Not because I didn't know the words, but because, for some reason, she couldn't make sense of them. I had to explain it again and again, slower each time, like I was talking to a child.

"No," I said. He's raping her. Right now!"

When she finally understood, she told me to call the police. I did. I gave the address. I said the words *domestic abuse* like I'd heard adults say them before, even though I didn't fully know what weight they carried, if any.

Concerned, Eugene put his hand around the bat he kept underneath the counter. "You need?" he offered in his Korean accent.

I just shook my head no, then I ran back.

When I reached the apartment, the sounds were still there— thudding, shouting, crying—all leaking through the door like something alive. I stood there listening, useless, holding nothing, my plan gone, my knife left behind.

My grandmother arrived before the police. That didn't surprise me. 911 ever moved quickly where we lived.

As she burst into the house, I heard a loud crash from behind the closed door in front of me.

"That was the sliding glass door," I said, narrating, as if she needed a play-by-play.

I heard my mother's exhausted voice pleading.

"Please—just let me put some clothes on."

When the door flew open, we were forced to look at one another.

She didn't look like my mother. She looked like someone who had been hollowed out and left standing in a daze. Her skirt was twisted, her top stretched, her hair wild. One eye was already swelling, the other one frantic and wide, like an animal caught in headlights.

The look that poured out from her was unbearable—encompassing everything at once: shame, fear, apology, and something worse—irreversible knowledge. The knowledge that I had heard it all. That her son had listened while she was violated.

Doug jumped the fence and ordered her to follow him—so she did.

"DIANNA!" my grandmother screamed, helpless and hoarse.

I ran outside to find Dion and Brianna playing near the laundry room with the other kids, laughing like nothing in the world was wrong. Latrice came running up first.

"Child," she said, breathless, "Doug got your mama on the other side of the fence. He pointin' a gun at her, too."

That's when I heard the Cadillac tear off through the grass.

I rushed Dion and Brianna to my grandmother's Chevy Blazer and shoved them into the back-back, the way we always did. They were crying now, asking questions I couldn't answer.

Inside the apartment, Mom-Mom was on the phone with the police, repeating herself.

"He's kidnapping her."

"I don't know."

"No, I don't know where."

She was losing time.

"Tell them his whole name," I said.

She paused, then said it.

I watched her face change.

"Yes—*that* Doug," she clarified. "Yes, him."

Her voice tightened. She didn't have to explain anymore.

"Tell them he's probably going to his mother's house," I added.

I knew they'd know exactly where that was. Pomona wasn't that big back then—especially not when it came to men like him.

Once we got into the Blazer, I yelled, "Let'sgo!"

"Go where?" she asked, from somewhere in a fog.

"To his mother's house!" I couldn't believe I had to say that.

"Snap out of it, Mom-Mom!"

She had just started the engine, and that's when the Cadillac came flying around the corner again, fast and reckless, tearing through the grass, then slowing gradually.

My mother jumped out of the car while it was still rolling.

I scrambled into the back seat as Doug came after her on foot, close enough to grab her hair again. She made it into the Blazer just as he reached us. The door slammed—but the window was still down.

He lunged through it.

We went feral.

I hit him. Scratched him. Bit him. My mother clawed at his face, his arms, his scalp. We pulled hair, skin—anything we could get our hands on. Nothing slowed him down.

"Drive!" I screamed.

"Drive!"

"Scrape him against the wall—just drive!"

The Blazer crept forward at a snail's pace, maybe a foot before stopping again.

That was when he got the door open.

He yanked my mother out by her earrings, tearing the holes in her ears into slits. I felt that pain in my own body. I grabbed her shirt with everything I had, felt the stitches give way as we pulled her back and forth like a rope in a game I couldn't win.

Then she stopped fighting.

I knew what that meant.

He had a gun, for sure. I couldn't see it, but I knew—the shift in her body, the way survival took over. She let go.

So, I did too.

I watched helplessly as he forced her back into the Cadillac.

The car smelled like him afterward, and so did I—sweat, dirt, cheap cologne. My mouth tasted like Jerry Curl juice from having his head between my teeth. My hands were greasy. My lip was bleeding. A knot was already rising on my forehead.

We sat there too long.

Too quiet.

"DRIVE!" I screamed again.

This time, she did.

When we pulled up to Doug's mother's house, the police were already there.

The Cadillac was pinned into the driveway at an angle, boxed in by two cruisers like an animal caught in a trap. Officers had Doug on the porch with guns drawn. Loud, sharp commands circled in the air amid the blue and red lights.

He looked smaller somehow. Still dangerous, still sweating, but no longer in control.

In my head, I wanted them to shoot him. I wanted it to end right there, permanently. Jail didn't feel like enough. Jail was familiar territory for him. Jail was just a pause.

It wasn't justice; it was an interruption. I wanted something permanent, something that matched what he had taken. But the police drove off with him anyway, and just like that, the immediate danger was gone.

Or so it seemed.

The ghost of that day stayed with all of us.

My mother was forever changed by that day.

Whether she knew it or not, my mother was forever changed by that day. Something essential inside her wilted—something that never fully came back. I saw it in the way she moved afterward, in what she no longer reached for, in the parts of herself she quietly laid down and never picked up again.

If time were to give me one more chance, I would go back to that night.

I would return to the moment just before she left us—just before she walked out the door and trusted the wrong instinct. I would make a scene so dramatic she couldn't ignore it. I would beg her not to go. I would tell her I was terrified that something terrible would happen if she left. I would threaten to burn the place down, to call 911, to wake the neighbors—anything to stop her.

I'd have taken the beating of a lifetime.

Whatever punishment came my way, I would have endured it if it meant sparing her the violence that was carved into her that night.

I would have sacrificed myself without hesitation, because by then I already believed that it was my role.

To absorb the damage, to stand between it and the people I loved, to carry what the adults could not or would not.

But in reality, none of it was my responsibility, and even though I was keen on taking the blame, none of it was my fault.

I was only a child.

# POMP & CIRCUMSTANCE

I took the city bus every morning for three years to Marshall Junior High School, all the way across town. Why, I have no idea. It was $1.10 for a round-trip transfer ticket, which included all the cussing, fighting, spitting, groping, and unwanted genital exposure any boy could handle in a single day. Honestly, that experience deserves a book of its own, so I'll save it for later.

Pomona High School was in yet another city. My mother wouldn't let me go to Ontario High, which had a bus to pick me up, lockers for my books, and two freaking swimming pools, and was about fifteen minutes away.

She worked for the Pomona Unified School District, so this way, she—and her new best friend, the Holy Ghost—could monitor me closely.

Since my mother was chronically late, I rode with my grandmother every morning. She worked at Garey High in Pomona. For four years, we carpooled, talked about the future, laughed, sang, and sometimes just sat in silence. I rarely missed a day. My high school experience seemed to fly by before I could even settle into it.

Now at its end, standing there on the risers, shoulder to shoulder, singing my balls off with the rest of the choir, my heart filled with something I wouldn't fully understand until later that day. I let myself feel all of it anyway. I soaked it in. There was a newness to it, something that hovered close to regret, but not quite. Not the regret of having done something wrong, but the kind that comes from knowing this might be the last time. The kind you feel when you realize you didn't cherish a moment while you were still inside it.

So I stood there, still, wrapped in a state of effortless reverence, letting everything exist exactly as it was. The way it does on the last day of school—when everyone signs your T-shirt with a marker, misspellings and all, and you don't correct a single one because getting it right was never the point anyway.

We had already sung You'll Never Walk Alone, now it was time for me to play with the band. My band. The band that I baked about a million cakes and cookies for so that we could raise enough money to afford buses for away games.

The band that I conducted at rehearsal, marched with, changed clothes in front of, screamed at, sweated with, cheered with, and laughed with.

We were the ones who jumped back off the bus to beat the shit out of some smart-mouthed, uppity band in San Diego at the Maytime Band Review together.

These were my people. They all knew me at my most musical, my most beautiful me.

This was to be the last song I ever played with them. From start to finish, it all came so quickly without even a flicker of déjà vu.

We played this song every year, rolling our eyes because it

repeated so many times from the last measure back to the beginning and over again until the final graduate crossed the stage.

But today, there wasn't a trace of boredom in me. Full of pride, I played as many measures as I possibly could that day. That last day. That last time. Then a few more. Then one more. Then just one last one.

Then it was my time to stand up to leave them. I couldn't smile —because that would've caused tears to break loose and slide down the outline of my face.

Instead, I kept the Horn Line Sergeant's mean mug on, the one they remembered from when it was time to handle business out on the grinder.

The same face that had them dropping for five hundred push-ups by the end of band camp. The same calm, unmoved expression I wore when we won sweepstakes. The one that reminded them not to celebrate like luck-struck *Price Is Right* contestants, because we weren't lucky.

We had worked harder than everyone else because we had less.

We had earned it.

That was the face I gave them as I stepped away.

I blew them a kiss and gently placed my French horn on its chair.

The principal called my name: *"Paul Allen Whitmore The Second."* I shook her hand. The auditorium roared. Mrs. Schroeder, my choir director, handed me a mock diploma, her arms flying open to embrace me, eyes shining. "You did it!" She said.

Freshman year, my mother had come to school to spy on me— normal, right? She caught me in tight green Levi bell-bottoms and a yellow Converse t-shirt with Kareem Abdul-Jabbar on the front.

A serious offense against our new Pentecostal, born-again way of life—showing off my ass and all. I had to hide the clothes at my friend Shawn's house so I could smuggle them in.

She grabbed me by the throat, pressed me against the wall, and shouted, "What the hell are you wearing?" Luckily, Mrs. Schroeder intervened, shaming my mother's fingers from my throat, walking her off campus.

From that day, Mrs. Schroeder knew a part of my struggle she hadn't before—the part that made me sing the way I did, the part Mr. Garrett had always understood.

Mr. Garrett conducted our little band as if it were the London Symphony Orchestra. His smile and wink served as a private acknowledgment. He knew the magic I could conjure with music. He had guided me all four years, ensuring I knew my own power. All I had to do was walk across that stage, and I was free.

My family was small—mother, grandmother, brother, sister— and I had only five tickets for an auditorium of over five hundred graduates.

Applause and whistles filled the room, but my happiness was real this time. I wasn't pretending.

Then his voice cut through: "Yeah, Paul-AYYY!" My father. Standing in the aisle, arms outstretched. Half audience, half spectacle.

"THAT'S MY SON!"

I wasn't smiling. I was pissed. He ran over and swung me around once, then again. I clenched my jaw, thinking:

*If your sorry ass had been around these last four years, people would already know I'm your son, fool!*

I had to escape.

When he let me go, I bolted, graduation gown flowing like a moody drag queen down Santa Monica Boulevard. I ripped off my tie, freed my neck, and my legs carried me right out of the building.

Family obligation and undeserved respect loomed over me like vultures circling, and I wanted none of it.

Not anymore.

# RUN PAUL RUN

$\mathcal{I}$ had to get as far away from Bridges Auditorium as quickly as possible. I took long strides powered by the intense, steaming resentment of a pissed-off teenage boy—and let me tell you, that kind of anger adds speed.

Before I knew it, I was crossing another parking lot, and at the far end I saw an oval-shaped grassy area. Having no clue where I was, I stomped right over the grass in defiance, then turned right and headed south.

If I could just figure out how to get to the main street outside the college, I could head west. I could walk and walk and walk until I reached the ocean, clear my mind, then make a plan or something. But the ocean was so very far—too far to walk, that's for sure.

My head bubbled with questions and regrettable scenarios. *How can I get to New York? Or Paris? I have no money, no car—shit, my mother wouldn't even let me get my driver's license.*

*I was fucked. I guess I could get fucked for money. At least it would be my choice, and I'd get paid for it. Save my money. Leave this city, these people, this stupid place forever.*

*But what about food? I don't need food.*

*And where would I sleep? Who cares.*

*Even if I had money, I couldn't get a hotel room—I didn't have an ID, and I wasn't eighteen yet...*

"Aye."

Out of nowhere, I heard a sexy Cholo accent.

Great.

"Congratulations, lil' homie!"

Someone shouted from behind the back side of a wall I was walking past, so gleefully that it irritated me. I stopped in my tracks, closed my eyes, whipped my head around, and fixed my mouth to say some smart-ass shit.

But when I opened my eyes, he was *fine*. Like *fine*-fine. DAAAAAAYUM fine.

He had to be somebody's uncle, cousin, or big brother or something, because he was over in the cut, doing the prison-picture squat, smoking a joint—and he knew about the graduation.

Clear olive skin. Sharp nose. Deep-set brown eyes beneath a strong brow. As if that weren't enough, his full, thick lips—outlined by a neatly trimmed, semi-thin goatee—had me instantly mesmerized.

Thick black hair combed back with that Tres Flores shine. Black-and-white Nike Cortez on his feet, and I could tell his gray khakis were brand new because the creases weren't faded yet—freshly starch-pressed, sharp enough to cut your finger on.

A gray-and-black checkered Pendleton buttoned only at the top, the rest spread open to reveal a crisp white T-shirt underneath, clinging to his thick pecs and framing his 12th Street neck tattoos. And to top it all off, a teardrop under his left eye.

Well now. Who was so kind as to send me an Aztec warrior as a graduation present? *This* is more like it.

So, thinking like any horny teenage boy, I thought, *Fuck it.*

Fuck all this other stupid shit I'm going through right now. I can keep running away *after* whatever this turns out to be.

Almost instantly, a smile spread across my sourpuss face like the sweetest honey on warm toast. He was an Aztec warrior. Staring past his beautiful eyelashes, directly into the sincerity of his eyes, I said, "Thank you."

He locked eyes with me, carrying a familiar, welcoming seriousness. When he stood, I saw he was much taller than I was—around six-foot-two, solid shoulders, no ambiguity left in his frame.

Then, in slow motion, he used his velvety pink tongue to lick his lips and sucked in a huge drag from the joint, the cherry glowing reddish-orange and black.

A small plume of smoke escaped his mouth before drawing it back in, chest heaving, head tilting back—all while keeping his eyes locked on mine.

"Come hit this shit?" he beckoned.

I was hypnotized beyond an obscene amount—and happy to be. He nodded with a wink, inviting me closer. I took two steps forward and was rewarded with his scent.

Drakkar Noir.

*Damn.*

I couldn't tell yet if there was any chance we'd make out, so if this was going to be the only way my lips ever touched something his lips had touched, I was more than okay with that.

I pulled myself together, refocused, tried to look cool—to look grown. Just to be certain our fingers touched for as long as physically possible, I made taking the joint from him into a whole production, pinching it deliberately, purposefully, imagining my fingers as a roach clip like the ones I'd seen dangling with feathers and beads from some auntie or uncle's rearview mirror.

As I brought it to my lips, he cracked a wickedly sexy yet shy, boyish smile, bobbed his head, and closed his eyes like he could feel the bass thumping from a lowrider on gold Dayton's, cruising through the hood in his mind.

*OOOOOH, he likes me.*

My thoughts went wild. *Don't fucking choke, you pussy. Don't ruin it. Be a mothafuckin' man, motherfucker!* But don't take too big a hit either—what if I get too high?

Ah, fuck. Here we go.

Why do I fucking care so much about *everything*? Maybe I should smoke more weed. Maybe then all the shit with my parents wouldn't make me so crazy. Maybe I could stay living at home, go to the thirteenth grade at Mt. SAC, drive some hooptie forever, and everything would just be easy.

Right?

*Oh my God—snap the fuck out of it, bitch. Baby hit. Just a baby hit.*

A car engine started behind me, followed by voices cheering and carrying on—normal kids who'd just graduated high school or something. They were happy. I was irritated. They were young and free, and I was old and tired already.

*Thanks a lot. Boner killers.*

If all these people kept coming around, I was never going to get to make out with this deliciously hot man—on my graduation day, outside Bridges' beautiful auditorium, beneath a manicured bottlebrush tree, pressed against a freshly painted, non-graffitied, gleaming white-ass wall.

Or do anything else, for that matter.

So I took only a baby hit. Holding the smoke in, I blurted out, while getting one last look at his face, "Thank you, but I gotta go."

He sucked his teeth in mellow objection.

"Where you goin'?" he grinned—that flirtatious grin that men give when they know there's at least a *chance* they could get some head.

"I have no freakin' idea," I muttered, handing back the joint, shoving my hands in my pockets, shaking my head, and resuming my speed walk south—toward who the fuck even knows where.

It seems that when you don't know where you're going, you can wind up there pretty damn fast.

I'd run away once before, the time my mother choked me for saying I didn't believe in God.

That time I walked in my socks, all the way from Ontario to my best friend's house in Pomona, down Holt Blvd. That time, she had the whole damn world looking for me. I wondered what would happen now.

It had only been about ten minutes, but I was already at Mills Avenue, heading toward the cemetery, almost to the 10 freeway. Maybe I could hitch a ride.

Yeah. Right.

*First of all, Paul, where the hell are you going? Second, you're dressed in a white linen vest, white flared linen pants, a peach dress shirt, and a peach-and-baby-blue tie—in the middle of Pomona—looking like The Great Gatsby trying to get into a stranger's car.*

*They'll turn your ass out and have you hookin' on Mission and Ramona. Bitch, think.*

But I couldn't think anymore. My brain hurt. I was exhausted —from thinking, from running, from believing escape was the only solution.

So I stopped, turned around, and walked back.

Truly, I wanted to stand and fight.

*I've been fighting all these years—what's a few more weeks?*

High school was over. I was done. I just had to figure out how to get to one of the six schools where I'd been accepted.

And therein lay the dilemma.

When it comes to Dianna, it is never easy. It is never "all I have to do." When you live under the rule of a mean-spirited, controlling, religious mother, nothing is ever simple.

When I got back to the auditorium, everyone was standing in the parking lot, near the door I'd escaped from earlier.

As I approached, my friend Merritt and his beautiful wife, Caroline, wrapped me in a group hug—I hadn't even known they were there.

They were the only two people from that church who saw through my mother's façade and reached out to help me, asking nothing in return.

They could tell I was always distraught—my mother trying to exorcise the gay demons out of me every chance she got—but they loved me through it, distracting me with hugs, kisses, and praise, just like they always had.

They taught me how to reach out to people who needed reaching. Though they may not have known it, the couple was an enigma—comfortably out of place wherever they were. I wanted to be that bold. Fiercely cool. Effortlessly confident.

Merritt was thin, tall, and muscular, with a chiseled chin and sharp nose. His smile beamed with perfectly straight white teeth. He had the swagger of a confidently cool, self-proclaimed nerd—graduated from Rice University in Texas—and he helped me fill out my application so I could get accepted there, too.

Caroline was sassy, her smile just as radiant. She had fine, straight black hair that, in proper 1990s fashion, was always bump-curled under and parted to the side. Always En Vogue—lean, tall, chic. Graceful, college-educated, always laughing.

When I told them I was attracted to other boys, they were the only people who said I was perfect just the way I was—and that anyone who judged me for being gay was not looking out for my best interest.

Their presence in my life feels almost angelic. One day they were there—so special to me—and then, *poof*, they were gone. Years passed before I heard from them again. I thought of them often and still miss them to this day.

Merritt was the big brother I should have had, but you don't get to pick your family, or do you?

# JUST LEAVE

No one seemed upset—or even aware—that I had been missing, so I didn't ask how long they'd been waiting. My father wasn't there either, which suited me just fine.

Mentally, I sent him back to whatever cornfield he'd crawled out of and didn't ask about him at all.

Other people's parents clustered together, talking about their kids—remembering booster meetings, games, performances, and the parties they were throwing that night.

My mother had nothing to add. She'd missed all of it anyway, and none of these people belonged to her church, so she couldn't give two shits about them or their memories.

Carloads of newly unenslaved kids drove by, yelling out windows, asking what I was doing that night. If I wanted to come over. If I wanted to ride with them.

"Git in!"

"Come on, Paul!"

I thought, *damn—now you fuckers invite me?*

I stayed cool. I could feel Dianna's eyes burning a hole through the back of my head.

I lied and told them my family was throwing me a huge party. Sorry. Can't go. Since my mother could see but not hear, she walked over and announced it was time to get in the car.

"Aye-aye, Captain."

I clicked my heels and gave her a crisp, sarcastic salute.

She hated that.

On the ride home, Dion and Brianna bubbled over with excitement about something, but I barely heard them. My mind was already racing ahead—toward freedom. And I was terrified I'd already taken two steps backward.

I feared that first awakening would fade, that I'd slip right back into my oppressive containment.

When we pulled up to the house, all the lights were off. We never did that. If you live in Pomona, you always leave a light on so people think someone's home.

So I thought: *Either this is a surprise party, or we're about to walk into a ransacked house.*

Good news: we hadn't been robbed.

Bad news: we hadn't been robbed.

The lights flipped on, and a roomful of old, Bible-clutching Deacon Mosses and Sister Esthers and Elder Jeremiahs shouted, "Surprise!"

It was all my mother's church people.

Please kill me now.

I smiled the way they liked me to and said, in my best *MTV's Daria* monotone, "Wow."

Strike three. They didn't notice.

I pushed through the sanctified well-wishes into the kitchen, where a homemade latex banner—my mother's handwriting, black and blue marker—stretched across the sliding glass door:

CONGRATULATIONS GRADUATES

DION & BRIANNA and Paul

Everything in capital letters.

Except my name.

Of course.

I was the only one in that house who had actually graduated from high school that day. Cap. Gown. Rehearsals. Song. Stage. Diploma. All of it.

Before I could react, my mother swooped in.

"I didn't want them to feel left out, so I put their names on the cookie cake too."

She opened the box like it was a grand reveal.

Perfect. Mediocrity, topped in frosting.

As I stood there absorbing the insult disguised as generosity, some long-winded West African deacon—Bilial, or Obadiah, or whoever—started drifting toward me.

Then the doorbell rang.

A sharp, deliberate knock.

*Well,* I thought, *I guess there is a Jesus.*

"I'll get it!" I shouted, already moving.

When my hand touched the doorknob, I stopped. Instinct kicked in. I knew who it was.

I backed away, turned calmly, and threaded through the praise-filled house into my room. I locked the door, then shoved the foot of Dion's twin bed against it.

I was furious—with him, but mostly with myself.

How dare I let this man stir anything in me? Who did I think I was, wanting more?

Did I really want a dad who showed up? Who cheered at track meets? Followed the band bus on Saturdays? Sitting in the audience, waving during choir concerts?

Yeah. I did.

I wanted the stupid stuff. The trivial stuff. The kind that makes a father, a son, and a little brother, *the boys.*

I wanted someone to show us how to sprawl on the couch, hand down our boxers, watching *Married with Children.*

Someone to box with real gloves. Someone to laugh louder than us when we burped or farted. Someone I could ask embarrassing sex questions without shame.

More than anything, I wanted a man I could look at and recognize myself in. A reflection. A lineage. A way to understand what kind of man I might become.

And maybe it was already too late.

Dion and Brianna must have let him in.

They ran to my door chanting, "Daddy's here!" I turned off the lights, locked myself in the bathroom, and turned on the fan.

Then his voice—outside the window. "It's Daddy. Come talk to me, son."

*Son.*

That word—after years of absence—felt like theft, embezzlement even.

Eventually, yet quite reluctantly, I came out.

"I got something for you, son."

I opened the door already armored. No hug. No smile. No sign of warmth.

He was standing too close.

I walked past him and out the front door. That's when I saw the white minivan—packed with strangers. Tina. Their kids. Halfway-house men.

A traveling circus to me. One that I wasn't going to join.

"They're not coming in here," I said flatly.

I looked up at the darkening sky and wished myself onto another planet.

Then I turned back to him. "Just leave."

# SON TO NO ONE

*I*nside, the angry little boy in me wanted my father to genuflect. To bow low in front of everyone and finally understand the gravity of his absence. I wanted him to beg—just a little—to stay at my party longer, to hear me out. To say the words *I'm sorry* loudly enough that the walls of my chest might finally crack and release some of what they'd been holding on to for years.

If he said them with enough force, maybe the sound alone could loosen the hurt lodged inside me. Like a healing earthquake strong enough to release the pressure so we could attempt—once more—to begin again.

In my fantasy, he would find the courage to speak honestly. To talk not as my father, but as a man who had once been a boy himself—abandoned by his own father—and who finally understood what that kind of leaving does to a child.

He would apologize for not knowing where I was from day to day. For never asking what scared me. For not knowing what happiness looked like on me.

He would apologize for all the times I braided my sister's hair before school. For the dinners I cooked after finishing my home-work. For squinting at Dion's chicken-scratch handwriting and making him erase it and do it again. For the laundry strung up on a clothesline, I had to rig myself. For scrubbing toilets and base-boards with bare hands until my skin burned—Comet, bleach, Pine-Sol soaked into my pores.

He would apologize for all the nights I swallowed fear because telling my mother about the men she brought around felt more dangerous than staying quiet. For the boyfriends. Their brothers. Their friends. The ones in the alley. The ones on the corner. All of them.

For being a soprano instead of a tenor. For mimicking my mother's voice so well, strangers commented on it.

For all of it.

He would apologize for never asking about the worst decision I had to make one night—never opening that door so the truth could breathe. Leaving me unheard. Unwanted. Unneeded. Unap-preciated.

Un, un, un,un,un!

Of all the *uns*, unheard is the most violent. Unheard creates the rest. Because when a child isn't truly heard, protection fails. The gates of the mind stay open. Fear moves in and furnishes the place with scary objects.

Love, I learned early, listens. Love hears. Love does something. Love acts. Love parents.

Imagine that.

If our roles had been reversed—if I were him and he were me —I would have shattered the moment open. I would have said *I'm sorry* a billion times and then one more. I would have listed every-thing through sobs and snot and the cracking of my voice until someone physically stopped me. Until someone physically covered my mouth, because I wouldn't know how to stop confessing.

I would have made damn sure he knew he was heard.

But instead, the night air of the San Gabriel Valley slipped between us, with its cool indifference. My father turned back toward me, cautious now, as if some unnamed fear had nudged him into motion. His long, tanned arms reached out slowly, almost reverently. He pulled me in.

I kept my arms pinned to my sides. Hands clasped tight below my stomach. No opening. No invitation. My jaw clenched. My brow lowered. I refused to let tears form in my eyes.

And yet—traitorously—I felt myself soften. The warmth of his chest. The familiar shape of him. His arms slid higher, around my neck. He kissed the side of my head. A few of his tears fell onto my face. I wiped them onto my lips. Tasted them. Kept them. Just so I could have something of him for myself.

"I do love you, son," he said.

Then that smile—the Pena Weenstraw smile that worked on everyone but my mother and me. He broke into song, crooning a few tired notes like music could rescue him.

It didn't.

I said nothing. Silence can sting worse than words if you let it. I wanted it to burn like lemon on a paper cut.

"Call me if you need anything, alright, son?"

*Anything? You owe me everything, Jack.*

He handed me a white envelope from his back pocket. Then he turned and walked away—toward the van full of people he *had* stayed for. He may have helped create me, but I wasn't anyone's clown.

Especially not his.

Almost on instinct, Dion and Brianna ran out to him. They soaked up the promises—sleepovers, trips to Knott's Berry Farm, all of it dependent on mommy's permission, of course.

Promises I'd heard before.

I called for them to come inside. Once. Then again. They

heard me. I know they did. But for that moment, they had him. And selfishly, I wanted to believe I was giving them that, though it wasn't mine to give.

They clung to him, drunk on the shine of our father's attention. The shade of his skin and Dion's matched so closely they looked like one person. And they were. And they weren't. Dion's eyes filled, and something hot burned up my throat. I wanted to punch my father square in his stupid, handsome face.

They didn't beg him to stay because they already knew better. That entitlement had been conditioned out of them.

I envied that they hadn't learned spite yet. That luxury had skipped me entirely.

I went back into the house, where the church people had transformed my graduation night into a revival: half tongues, half English. Full plates.

I closed my eyes in the kitchen and made a wish. A benevolent one, I think. I wished for the rapture they all were looking forward to so much to arrive immediately—right there, right then—so they could all float away, turn to dust, or vanish in robes and halos.

Whatever.

Just get the fuck out of this house.

# SUNDAY'S NEWS

The Sunday following my graduation, we—of course—had to go to that ever-loving, whooping-hollering, fake-ass church.

A so-called prophet from New York had been invited as a guest speaker, which meant one thing: boosting the offering. His job was to guilt anyone who hadn't been paying their tithes into reaching deep into their pockets until it hurt. That, they said, was when the real blessings come.

This Sunday would prove to be different. This one would matter more than any other. It was the tipping point—the hinge on which my entire future would pivot.

Every other Sunday followed the same grueling structure. At 7:30 a.m., my cousins Khalilah and Malita, my schoolmate Zakiyah, and I attended teen class over in Kid's Kingdom. At 9:30, we bolted for Lonnie and Greg's car to grab a donut before relocating to the main sanctuary.

At 10:30, the bodyguards—yes, bodyguards—opened the east-facing double doors so the pastor could step out of her green Jaguar or her gleaming white Rolls-Royce. Pink Chanel or cream

Adrienne Vittadini suit. Wireless microphone strapped on. She'd enter mid-verse like a headliner, gliding down the aisle as the choir carried her in.

The sermon would begin at 11:00 a.m. We were told it was the season of "Jubilee". Every service included the announcement that God was saying at least a few people in the audience needed to come forward and pledge $2,500—payable in four easy install-ments—as a sacrifice for a sick, unsaved, or wayward loved one.

Around 1:00 p.m., the tithes procession commenced with everyone dressed in their finery, hopeful to meet the pastor's fashion expectations.

One by one, we filed from the pews, guided by mostly over-weight ushers, balding not by choice, who gleefully directed human traffic toward the altar.

The mauve fabric-lined brass bucket waited at the front, held by some lucky guy close enough to the pulpit to inspect whether the glint on the pastor's self-announced Jimmy Choos came from rhinestones or plastic beads.

Behind her, a backlit 3D atlas glowed with the words *"Into All The World."*

We clapped and marched while she sang something catchy—*Jehovah Jireh, my provider...* Tambourines popped off like firecrack-ers, while Sister Berniece caught the Holy Ghost and fell out, as usual.

A woman of front-row royalty, sporting airbrushed acrylic nails, motioned for ushers to lower Berniece gently and drape her legs with a modesty cloth.

If her chest got covered that day, it was church code: *leave that tittie showin' blouse at home next time.*

Khalilah and I tried to believe. Just as often, we had to stifled our giggles by pretending to pray with our faces in our laps or by acting like we were reaching for something under the pew in front of us.

By two o'clock, our stomachs growled. By three, another offering. By four, the altar call—my cue to drag myself onto the stage and sing *As the Deer Panteth*, which always sounded like Dr. Seuss to me.

By then, my belly felt hollowed out. The adults told us that hunger meant the Spirit was moving through us. The closer you were to God, the emptier you felt.

These people had an answer for everything. All I could think was— *What the fuck?*

That day, unbeknownst to me, God had sent Prophet Bernard Jordan all the way from New York—2,761 miles and 5.7 billion people away—just to deliver a word for little ol' me.

After the service gained momentum, he spoke in gibberish tongues, then urgently called for all graduating young men to come forward.

We lined up under the congregation's gaze. He was tall, bald, big-headed, with a ghetto project-boy's lisp and a microphone held with the foam brushing his mouth. His eyes fluttered like he was receiving transmissions from Sky Daddy.

Barely looking at the others, this strange-looking, sneaky-acting weirdo came straight for me.

Right then and there, I knew that my mother and Pastor Carolyn were behind it.

Pastor Carolyn—the same woman who demonized "homa-sek-shulls" at nearly every service—loved to pose questions across the pulpit about what two men did in bed, as if she hadn't been a self-proclaimed coke-snorting, miniskirt-wearing prostitute in Maryland during the '60s and '70s.

Her sermons were never abstract. When she was speaking about homosexuality, she was talking directly to me. Everyone knew it. I was the only obviously gay boy in that whole place.

"God is moving," the prophet announced. "There's a young man here about to make the wrong decision."

He slathered my forehead with oil and delivered God's specific plan: stay home. Community college. No music. Get a job. Help with my mother's bills. Keep raising my siblings. As consolation, the church would provide a car.

Mt. SAC. Community College. Thirteenth grade.

My internal answer was immediate: *No way!*

I wanted to knee him right in the balls, then punch him when he folded.

But I played the same survival game that I always had. I raised my hands, fell back into Merritt's arms, as he lowered me down onto the mauve carpet, palms flat on the floor beside me, pretending to be slain in the so-called Spirit—a quick way to get this shit over with.

Merritt whispered, "Don't get mad. I'm right here."

The tears came anyway—not because of this fake God shit, but for my mother's betrayal. She must have sensed that I had an escape plan because I hadn't told her where I'd been accepted for college yet.

When I got home from that fucking place that day, I was done.

There are only a few good times in one's life when that kind of doneness happens, and for me, this was one of them. This was a stick-a-fork-in-me kind of done. I went into action by secretly organizing my things. I quietly placed my neatly folded shirts, pants, socks, and underwear into plastic trash bags, stowing some underneath my bed and some in the middle part of the closet, so that if you opened one side at a time, you couldn't see what was patiently lurking against the wall.

Dion started getting suspicious, though.

"Paulie, why do you keep putting those bags under your bed?"

Touché. A valid question, since I was the one always yelling at him for stuffing his dirty clothes under his.

"I'm just getting ready for when I have to go to college."

"But you aren't supposed to move out."

Dion had been learning from the sound technician how to operate the booth in "grown-up" church. No more Kids' Kingdom for him. Now he heard and saw everything that went on in there, and he was drinking the Kool-Aid—Great!

When he used the words *supposed to*, it ate at my nerves. I was supposed to move out. That's what people who go away to college do. I knew that if I argued with him or tried to make him understand the depth of what was happening to me, he'd run and tell our mom what he saw me doing. So I had no choice but to change the subject.

"Wanna use my tape recorder?"

"Yeah."

"Go ahead."

From then on, I resigned from my role as older brother and shut my ass up about telling him what to do. I had to start thinking only of myself now, which was difficult, to say the least.

All I had ever done in life was think first of my brother and sister and put myself last. I was the oldest. That was my job. Everyone said it was my job—but why? Why was it my fucking job to look after someone else's children when I too was a child? Because I could? Because I was good at it? Because my heart was true and loyal?

I had important problems to tackle. Like where I would live and how I would afford food. Would I be able to get wherever *there* was without a car? I didn't even have a driver's license. My age was the biggest problem I faced.

Well, not enough of it, to be exact. I was only seventeen, leaving another year before I was legally an adult. Guess who was brilliant at reminding me of that fact. Dianna was great at it.

"You can't do anything without my written consent."

She would sometimes say it with a snobbish smirk. And the *written* part—what parent says that so specifically? Most times, it was delivered in a domineering tone, flared nostrils and all, like a threat.

The fact of the matter was that I still had two parents. Two inept parents, but still two separate parents. No one had bothered to get a proper divorce after all those years anyway. No court orders. No custody rights. No child support. No nothing.

Good thing for me and my plan to leave.

On Monday morning, I found out I would be home alone for the day. Who knows—or remembers—where she took my brother and sister? I didn't care.

I went straight to my top drawer and opened the envelope my dad had given me. Just like I'd hoped, it turned out to be a card holding money—twenty whole dollars. Don't even ask me what the card said, because the moment I saw the money, all I thought was *Jackpot!*

I was gonna get fucked up.

Off to get some Strawberry Cisco and a blue Mad Dog 20/20 —whatever flavor that shit was. I drank it out of my sipper at school all the time.

My Algebra II teacher was an alcoholic, too. He drank coffee spiked with Baileys from an old Styrofoam cup, and his classroom was the perfect place for me to get away with my own daily, underage drinking.

Second period was the longest class of the day. It had an extra fifteen minutes built in. I used that to take it slow, to get tipsy enough to forget my life.

The guy at the liquor store next to the Jelly Donut had a thing for me, so he'd sell me alcohol before school.

He was an Indian guy in his twenties, pretty cute, too, but the fact that he didn't wear a lick of deodorant kept me exactly a flirt's distance away and not one squeak closer.

"Come back here so I can show you something."

"I can't. I have a boyfriend."

"A boyfriend? You come on back here—I'll be your boyfriend too."

To keep the door open, I'd leave it at, "I have to get to class." I'd smile and say things like, "See you after school," or "Maybe next time."

Getting drunk was my learned escape. I wondered if anyone even understood how drunk I needed to get.

I didn't know any other gay boys who went to a non-denominational Pentecostal church, who had a delusional and abusive mother trying to ruin their lives.

I was tired of endlessly winding around this small, twenty-mile-radius blip on Earth, tethered to my mother's version of God —her ridiculous rules, her newfound craft of weaving maniacal constructs, all in the name of Jesus.

As far as I was concerned, nobody needed a drink as much as I did. Her bullshit couldn't be all there was to life, and I knew it. I had always known it—from the inside.

I knew it when we had only three bath towels for five people, and whenever the electricity was cut off.

When we pretended it was a picnic while eating sandwiches for dinner because the gas bill hadn't been paid, because Daddy had smoked up his entire paycheck.

I knew it then.

Even as we stood in line, exposed to everyone outside the social security office on Ganesha and Holt for government eggs, cheese, flour, and milk, there was some soothing confirmation whispering in my ear, telling me this wasn't all there was to the fullness of life—or to living it.

The real living of it.

Living like someone who mattered to himself, like the people I watched on TV and in the movies.

Hopeful as I was about the future, the young man I was

becoming didn't yet know how to break through without getting a little tipsy first.

Sometimes I laughed to myself, wondering if this was what everyone around me imagined as the outcome of their own lives.

After a few swigs of that strong stuff, I was on cloud nine. Nothing bothered me. I felt light as a feather.

By the time my mom got home with Dion and Brianna that day, I was already nearing sobriety.

In between doing the laundry and taking the chicken out to defrost, I watched *The Grind* on MTV, played all the secular music videos on BET that I wasn't supposed to see, and jerked off about ten times.

I brushed my teeth, gargled, and practiced words—sprinkling in a few phrases I might be required to answer with, without slurring. *Yes. No. I already did. Okay.* Then I turned the living room TV to cartoons. That was safe.

Dion came into the house first, making a beeline for the kitchen. Brianna was right on his heels, as usual, making sure whatever he got, she got the same.

The smell of my mom's Giorgio by Giorgio Beverly Hills eau de toilette made it through the door well before she did.

Then came the familiar sight of her stepping inside with a school tote holding her Bible, her purse hooked in the crook of her left elbow, one clip-on earring clenched in her fist, the other dangling from a single ear, her keys tight in her right hand.

"Go get the rest of the bags out of the car."

This required no verbal response, so I was one for one on the no-talking front.

"Did you finish the laundry?"

"Yes," I said confidently, trotting out the front door.

We wouldn't have much time to eat, but we were used to that. It was Monday night prayer. That meant that by six o'clock we had to be on our way to church, since service started at six-thirty. We never missed it. Not ever.

She still had to change and fix her makeup, which meant, as usual, I would be the one making dinner.

She called out from her bedroom.

"Season the chicken, then cover it with some foil and put it in the broiler."

I whispered the last part along with her, rolling my eyes and shaking my head, the same way I always did.

"Just make some rice and string beans to go with it."

Once the chicken was in the oven, I moved through the kitchen the way I always did—quietly, efficiently, without thinking too much about whose job it really was. I put the groceries away, careful not to disturb the small things my mother claimed as hers.

Cream cheese. Salsa. Tortilla chips.

That combination was her version of self-care, and it was understood that it was not for us.

In one of our white cereal bowls with the blue stripe around the rim, she would soften the cream cheese in the microwave—never more than a minute—then stir in Pace Picante sauce and eat it slowly with tortilla chips until whatever craving she had finally loosened its grip.

I loved the notion of having anything just for myself. It had been growing ever since I started imagining college as more than school—as an escape.

As I opened the can of string beans and let the water drain into the garbage disposal, the thought arrived fully formed, without panic or hesitation.

I didn't need to go to prayer.

I needed to stay home.

And I needed to call my father.

He had told me to call if I ever needed anything. For once, I was going to hold him to the offer.

# THE ESCAPE

*A*naheim was much closer to Cal State Fullerton than Pomona was. If I lived with my dad, I could go to school there. I could stay with him for a semester, while I got used to it, then move into the dorms.

This would be easy. After all, I had already been accepted into the Summer Bridge program. This plan made sense in a way that most things in my life hadn't. But the logistics weren't the problem.

It was Dianna.

If Dianna found out, she would block it—just like she always had when something meant freedom for me. I already had enough credits to graduate in the eleventh grade, but she wouldn't allow that either. Not if it meant losing control. My future only mattered to her when it involved my labor or my compliance.

I was the sole contestant on a reality show called *Figure Out Your Fucking Future*, where every obstacle had been custom-built by my mother.

"Mom, I got accepted to the Orange County School for the Performing Arts. Can I go?"

No.

"I got accepted to audition for Juilliard."

No.

"I got accepted to Rice University in Texas."

No.

So this time, I wouldn't ask her. Instead, I would plan my great escape.

I would go to prayer that night. I'd wait until everyone was riled up in a tizzy. In the middle of all the cackling in tongues, the crying, rolling on the floor, laying hands on one another.

As soon as white boy Markus got that organ music cranked all the way up to eleven, and the whole place was jumpin', I'd make my move with one finger pointed to the sky, pretending to head to the restroom like nothing was up.

As soon as the door slammed shut, I'd run my little ass through the back parking lot at top speed, only slowing up enough to gauge my momentum for clearing the jump over that black wrought iron fence. Then straight over to the Taco Bell pay phone to call my dad.

Easy!

"Did you get the chicken in?" Dianna snapped me back into the now. It was like she knew exactly when to interrupt me.

"Yes, it's in.

I went straight to my room. On our last trip across the country, driving Route 66 through Oklahoma City, my grandfather had bought me a cedar treasure box with a tiny lock.

Inside my little lacquered box, I kept the few things that felt like mine. A folded picture of a handsome, barefoot International Male catalog model wearing some see-through onion-skin underwear; an unused ticket to *Madame Butterfly* from a failed date night, a note from a boy named Roman saying he loved me; and a pile of quarters scattered over everything like ballast.

I slipped the quarters into my right sock, then eased my foot in slowly, spreading them out so they wouldn't touch one another. No touching meant no noise. I just needed them to stay put on the walk to the car, in the car, and into the church.

"Let's hurry up and eat so we can leave. Go make the plates."

If it was an order, it was for me. I moved fast.

I didn't want to eat too quickly, but I wanted us out of the house even faster. The quarters had to stay quiet in my shoes.

"Can I have the ketchup?" Dion shouted.

"Please?" I corrected.

"Ntch—please!" He sucked his teeth, annoyed at being reminded.

"I want some too," Brianna added, right on cue.

My mom came into the kitchen, stretching a pair of nylons between her hands. "Are these stockings blue or black?"

"They're blue," I said, encouragingly, while thinking, *Can we just get the fuck out of here already?*

I didn't even want to eat anymore, but prayer could trap us there for hours, so I finished my plate. I washed it, dried it, and put it away like always. I didn't want to do a single thing out of the ordinary—nothing that could tip her off or derail my plan.

Dion and Brianna carried their plates to the sink after scraping the little they hadn't finished into the trash.

"Here, hand me those and go put your shoes on."

"It's time to go. Get in the car." Finally, she gave the all-clear.

I slid into the back behind the passenger seat, careful not to let Dianna see my face directly behind her. I didn't want her getting any ideas—no conversation, no new chore, no new rule. Especially not anything about the so-called prophecy.

She hadn't mentioned a word. Not a peep about the shift in the trajectory of my life, all orchestrated by what she was passing off as God's omniscient instruction. So far, there had been no mention of the promised car, applying to Mt. SAC, or finding a job.

No plan to make a plan. Perfect. I already had one. Little did she know she was nudging me closer to the payphone I needed.

Her little red Geo Metro whipped through the streets of Pomona until we reached the church parking lot. When we stopped, I bounced my foot quietly, testing the silence, preparing for the walk to the wooden doors.

Once inside, I would slip into the mother's section—back left, where the overhead lights stayed off—and sit close to the side exit nearest the restrooms outside. Perfect for a quick escape.

I made my way around the sound booth. I was stunned to see old Apple Head Jamal. Khalilah's ex-boyfriend was sitting right where I had planned to be. Jamal was a handsome, tall guy with green eyes and blondish-brown hair, cut in a Caesar with waves combed forward, and the best smile.

What on earth was he doing there anyway?

He had already graduated the year before me and hadn't been to Monday night prayer ever since. Besides, they lived all the way out in Compton.

Being flirtatious was his way of picking on me, amicably, and I must say that I didn't mind that. Tonight, I didn't have time for any foolishness, though, so I pretended like he wasn't even there.

I sat down three or four pews behind him. As soon as I sat, he raised his giant body, turned around, then gave me that look like —I know you saw me.

Sucking my teeth, I slid my body down to kneel like I was praying, facing the back of the pew.

"Scoot over." He said in his bass of a voice. There he was, right there next to me on his knees, pretending to pray too.

"You scoot over, Jamal."

"Why you mad at me? What'd I do?" Changing positions, he sat down properly, facing forward, eyes closed, with both hands together touching his nose in a prayer position.

"Nothing! I'm not mad at you." I whispered.

"You can't say hi to a brotha?"

"Hi," I said, keeping my eyes closed with hands clasped.

"Dang, attitude!"

"Jamal, be quiet! I need to sneak out and call my dad over at the Taco Bell payphone, but my mom can't know."

"Okay. Are you okay?"

"Yeah. I'm fine."

"Just chill, calm down, man." I must have sounded frantic.

He understood without me having to go into detail. After all, he had once been a fellow detainee. All the teenagers at Word Harvest Worship Church shared a common understanding that we didn't really know what the hell these grown-up people were trying to do to us, so we had to stick together.

Jamal also knew about that year he'd walked in on me and the guy who kissed me in the men's bathroom during Hallelujah Night.

Yes, the hilariously saintly alternative to Halloween—and the bane of every church teen's existence. Everyone dressed as biblical characters, played games, and got free candy.

In the middle of my stalling his attempt to lock lips, the guy grabbed me and went all in before I could even decide if I was okay with it.

Just as the surprise of how nice his lips felt started to sink in, the door popped open. Jamal appeared, dressed as someone who might have herded a few donkeys through a field in Bethlehem, back in 22 B.C.

He calmly entered the tiny, now crowded bathroom, shut the door behind him, maneuvered past us, and spoke over the sound of the stream flowing into the commode:

"Everybody's looking for you."

The other guy bolted like the wind.

"Looking for who?" I asked.

"You."

"What for?"

"I don't know."

And that was that. As far as I knew, he never told another soul about the kiss. If he did, it never came back to me. I trusted Jamal.

Tonight, I just had to get out before it got too late. Time crawled, my anxiety building, until one of the men jumped on the drums and Markus, our German pianist, took to the organ. Sister Berniece made her way to the stage, grabbed the microphone, pointed at the congregation, and began to sing:

"You cain't curse what God has blessed, no matter how hard you try."

This was my moment. I stood and sang like someone who meant it, eyes closed for added effect. Jamal rose too. Chaos was about to break out in the name of Jesus, and that was exactly the cover I needed. I scanned the congregation, finding my mother, so I could avoid her gaze.

Sister Berniece carried on:

"You see everything you touch; it turns to gold. And baby, lemme tell you the reason why. Cause you cain't curse what Go-hod, Go-a-ahd has ble-heh-hessed."

"Go!"

Jamal nudged my shoulder. I squeezed past him, as he called after me: "Ay, bring me back some cinnamon twists."

# MISSION TO ANAHEIM

While the church repeated the chorus, I took my chance and, like a thief in the night, I was out the door in a flash. Running at top speed to the corner of the gate, I hoisted myself over with all the stealth I could muster.

Anyone watching from the apartments across the street probably would have cheered anyway—they knew how long we were cooped up in that place for hours on end.

All I could hope for was that the payphone wasn't in use. Of course, some little kid was already on it—cut-off shorts, black tank top, flip-flops, shiny jacket slung over one shoulder.

Tap, tap, tap. I knocked on the glass.

"Please, I'm so sorry, but I have an emergency. I have to call my dad."

No luck there. The "kid" turned out to be a short, sassy, older queen whose ashy legs hadn't seen a single pump of Jergen's lotion in days.

He looked me up and down, snapped his fingers, then smiled through the glass, and said, "Oh girl, I'm so sorry, but I have to call my daddy too, boo-boo!"

I rolled my eyes, mouth slack. Then I noticed a lady in a Taco Bell uniform on the other side of the glass.

"You need a phone, baby?"

"Yes, Ma'am," I said, urgency in my voice.

"Come on wit' me."

I shot the old man a look as we walked past the phonebooth. He turned his head away, palm to the glass, as I mouthed back to him, *Old, funky-ass bitch.*

Once we entered her office, this kind young lady asked, "Everything alright?" The real answer was no, but I couldn't tell her that.

"I just have to call my dad and ask him to come get me."

She removed her hat, letting her extensions fall, as she shook out her hair, and patted her scalp like she'd been waiting all night to do it.

I sat at the phone and picked up the receiver. "Imma be right out here," she said, before stepping back outside, cigarette in hand.

I dialed quickly, waiting impatiently. Every ring stretched out like an eternity. *What if he wasn't there? What if the line was discon-nected?* My patience was thinning.

"Hello?"

"Hi, Daddy."

"Wally Gator? Hey son, I'm so glad to hear your voice."

"Daddy, I have to ask you something."

"Okay."

"Listen. I'm sneaking to call you because I can't let Mom know."

"Okay," he said cautiously.

"She won't let me go to college because a prophet said I had to stay home and help with the bills."

"Who said that?"

"Prophet Bernard Jordan," I said, rushing.

"That fuckin' sissy ain't no prophet, son."

"I know, Daddy, but she's not letting me go. I think she and Pastor Carolyn asked him to say that."

"Okay, son. Tell me what you want me to do."

"I got accepted to Cal State Fullerton, and since you're close there in Anaheim, I thought I could live with you."

"So you want to come live with me?" I could hear a smile in his voice.

"Yes."

"Okay, son. When do you need me to come get you?"

"Can you come on Saturday? The bridge program starts next week. I just have to show up with my paperwork."

"I'll be there Saturday morning around nine."

"Okay, I have to go. Thank you, Daddy."

"Call me Friday night to touch base."

"I will. Thank you, Daddy! Bye."

I yelled a quick thanks to the Taco Bell lady as I ran out the back door, hoisted myself back over the gate, and discovered—it had been left open the whole time.

I sprinted across the lot to the church storage warehouse, slowing to a clandestine trot to catch my breath before switching to a brisk walk.

I reached the brown double doors of the sanctuary. Pressing my nose to the wood, peeking through the crack, I saw the congregation assembled at the altar, praying for someone I couldn't identify. Hopefully, it wasn't Jamal—my mother would have noticed I wasn't sitting next to him.

I eased the door open and slipped inside, moving quickly to the stage. Don in the sound booth gave me a thumbs-up; Dion was with him, easily distracted, so I remained unnoticed. Next to the piano, I saw exactly who they were praying for: Sister Dianna, shoeless, in blue stockings, a floral dress flared to one side, her French Roll unraveling, and crying. Her body flattened out like road kill on the 91 freeway. I let out a disdainful tooth-suck. Whatever—she had no clue I'd sneaked out.

My plan had worked. Freedom was imminent, so nothing she could do would matter for the next few days. Five more to be exact, and I'd be gone. Peacocking inside with secret satisfaction, I remembered the quarters in my sock. I went over to one of the mics, then I blended in by opening my mouth to join in on the cultish ridiculousness, biding my time, singing:

Bless the Lord,

Oh my soul…

# MISSION ACCOMPLISHED

From start to finish, the morning after I made my escape plan was one of the easiest, most carefree I could remember.

I slept so well that the morning came to me for once, instead of me having to come to it. My sleepy eyes drifted back to consciousness slowly, lit from behind by an orange-colored glow pressing through my eyelids.

It was hella quiet—carpeted-room quiet, with the California sunshine spilling through the window, warming not just my face but the entire top half of my twin bed.

The kind of quiet that feels almost suspicious, where you have to shift your body or clear your throat to make sure your ears still work. I woke to find the house empty again. For the second day in a row, by some form of miracle, I had slept through the inconsiderate ways of those bumbling people I lived with, too. It took them forever to get the fuck up. Like, to rise and shine? Forget it.

Every morning, each of them uttered the same tired phrase, "I need to thaw out." It was enough to make teenage hormone-raging me want to slap them all.

Dianna had to have her stupid cup of coffee while she sat there, holding the handle in one hand with the other wrapped around the base, hunched over somewhere like a patient from One Flew Over The Cuckoo's Nest.

Dion always stayed in bed until he had barely enough time to put his clothes on and eat.

And then there was little Brianna, wrapped in some blanket, covering her head, tucked under her chin, while staring into the distance like a catatonic nun.

Just wake the fuck up already, people!

After all the closet opening, toothbrushing with the water running, and the drawer slamming started, all of their reverence for the peaceful morning they clung to so dramatically went right out the window.

The only other time I had slept this well was the night after I found out that Dianna knew, undeniably, that I was being gay with a boy from school. Regularly. No other person on earth has ever slept that good, lemme' tell you.

They must be going to summer school, is what I was thinking, but believe me, I didn't fucking care. Not one inch. Finally! I didn't give a shit about what anyone else in this house, on this street, this planet, or this galaxy was doing.

Do whatever the fuck you want bitches because I'm outta here. This must have been what everyone else felt like all the damn time. The whole world, giving zero fucks about absolutely no one aside from themselves. Fuck 'em!

So, I made Aunt Jemima pancakes with cinnamon and sugar mixed in, covered with peanut butter and strawberry preserves, some lightly done turkey bacon, scrambled eggs with melted cheese on top, and a bowl of cereal. Yes cereal! With sugar! And, I didn't even have to beg my mother to have it because she wasn't fucking there!

I couldn't wait to repeat all the mild debauchery I had

indulged in freely just the day before. If this were life without these folks around, I wanted it 24/7. For real!

No sneaking, no hiding. Listening to the music of my generation whenever I wanted. Some Jodeci or Monica with a fresh beat and a new groove I could dance to.

My ears had become waxed over with the tired-ass sounds of church ladies who made songs to Jesus sound more like love ballads to some man they were hoping would propose marriage to them.

Or the closeted church homo's who liked to sing about how God had scooped them up in just the nick of time. Scooped them up from what? From suckin' another dick or two? Come on!

I knew what I would be up to from now on—finally doing me. I wouldn't have to hide my journals under my mattress anymore or keep the main ones with all the cuss words and dirty drawings, at school, in my band folder tucked away in my cubby.

I just had to make it to Saturday without getting into any riffs or squabbles with Dianna, but I hadn't figured out exactly how to tell her that I had already dropped the axe on her little plan to keep me prisoner.

Speaking to her calmly wouldn't work. The conversation would start with me politely asking if I could talk to her about something, but her usual response was, "About what?"

Never, "What's on your mind, honey?" or "Is everything alright?" I'd have to pretend I was worried or confused, hoping that would inspire some softness from her otherwise calloused approach to parenting.

No matter how many times I tried that, it never worked anyway. This time, I would be forthcoming and honest.

I'd do it respectfully, because I wasn't about to let her spin a version of the story into me being childish or rude. Even though I'm pretty sure that's how she'd tell her sisters in Christ about it.

I had a plan: on Saturday morning, before my dad arrived, I'd gather all my things, line them up against the wall at the front door, then call for her. When she asked what I was doing, or more accurately, what I *"thought"* I was doing. That's when I'd explain with something like:

"I know you want me to stay home, go to community college, and work, but..." or

"When the prophet said..." or

"I don't think God would have let me get accepted to all those colleges if..."

I had to face it. No matter how much of a refreshing scent I sprayed over my words, or how nicely I put it, none of those approaches would work, and I knew that. I knew her better than anyone on earth.

I'd been with her since she was sixteen years old. Watching her. Day after day, year after year, as she changed into an adult, with me growing at a rate not far behind her.

When she turned twenty, twenty-five, thirty, I was there. I was the largest consequence of her adolescent folly, me, now all grown up and trying to get my neck out from under her boot.

"I'm moving in with my dad so I can go to college." That's what I would say, flat out. That was it. The truth without additives, without an apology. Spoken directly, with absolution in my tone, I would share with her the plain truth, and if she didn't like it, then she could just go fucking pray about it in a corner somewhere.

And while she was at it, maybe she could ask that psychic prophet why he didn't see that one comin'.

Whether she would accept it or not, it was time. Time for me to take control of my life. Tuesday was now coming to a close without a hitch, so now it was two down, three and a wake-up to go.

On Wednesday afternoon, I was in my bedroom when they all got home. I heard Dion and Brianna arguing over who had more of whatever they were eating, and the shower across the hall was going.

My mother was getting herself ready before church. She'd have to bathe, do her makeup, get dressed, and curl the ends of her hair—all that shit, so I had a little time to make a phone call to my dad before she ordered me to get ready to leave.

Questioning whether or not he'd show up on Saturday made me antsy.

Calling only the night before wouldn't help soothe my nerves either, so I had to reach him tonight. A couple of days before, just to set my mind at ease. After all, reliability had not been a superlative that came to mind when referring to Paul Whitmore Sr.

I pushed the edge of Dion's bed frame in front of the door, then pounced over to the phone.

Picking up the receiver, I waited, listening for any sounds in between the dial tone so I could hear if someone else picked up another phone in the house.

After dialing, I listened impatiently to the sound of a phone on the other end of the line just ringing and ringing.

For this plan of mine to work, my dad had to do what he said he would, which had never happened before. Otherwise, I was to be stuck there with my mom forever in a gay-hell nightmare.

Then someone finally answered.

"Hello."

"Can I speak to my dad, please?"

"Who is this?"

"This is little Paul. Can I please speak to my dad please?"

"This is Tina."

Wow, she knew who she was! That was promising. Maybe she could even spell it, too. Now, I just had to penetrate her thick, empty skull enough to get her to understand that I wanted to speak to my dad and not to her.

"Good…You're Tina, and I'm little Paul. Can you put my dad, Big Paul, on the phone now, please?"

Annoyed, she yelled out, "Paul!" "Phone!"

"It's little Paul. He has a funky attitude." Humph, got her!

"Hey, son."

Hi Daddy. "I can't talk for very long because Mom is home. Are you still coming on Saturday at nine?"

"I'll be there, son."

"Daddy…"

"What?"

"Please don't leave me hangin' this time. This is serious."

"I'll be there. I promise."

"I have to go. I love you." I said that so easily after all these years of withholding those three words at bay as punishment. If I had surprised myself that much, I know he was surprised too.

It probably even melted a bit of his heart, but I couldn't stay on the phone long enough to find out, so I just hung up with my index finger, carefully sliding it out while replacing it with the handset.

Mission accomplished.

# FAGGOT, FAGGOT, FAGGOT

Sitting quietly on my bed, I studied Cal State Fullerton's glossy, in-color, full-page welcome packet — the one I hid under my mattress. The campus map, parking instructions, addresses, phone numbers, and unfamiliar building names overwhelmed me—McCarthy Hall, Langsdorff Hall, The Fullerton Arboretum.

I didn't see anything that looked like a music building, but maybe it was hidden inside one of these halls.

Still fearful of God and the mumbo jumbo of the false prophecy, I'd already decided to avoid anything having to do with orchestral music. So I thought I'd found a loophole by studying Dance instead.

"You guys ready?"

Dianna's voice carried down the hall — "Wednesday night Bible study in a few minutes."

Oh shit. I couldn't remember where my damn Bible was.

Not on the bookshelf. Not on the dresser. Maybe I left it in the living room. Shit. I probably kicked it under the front seat of the car when I got out Monday night. If it were there, I couldn't ask her for the keys anyway. That would mean admitting I hadn't read the prescribed daily Psalm and Proverb.

She'd know the magical book had been sitting there, locked up, baking in the heat, screaming for fresh air — wedged between the floor and the metal workings of the seat.

I'd have to sneak out, check if the car was unlocked — highly unlikely — then sneak it back inside just so I could turn around and walk out the door holding it, passing the first-glance inspection from Frau Dianna Himmler, Bible Nazi.

Too late.

The usual makeshift barrier against my door hadn't held. I sprang up from the bed to face my mother.

"Where's your bible?" She preened in her signature accusatory tone — which meant she already knew exactly where my fucking Bible was.

"I think I left it in the car Monday night."

"You think?" Her eyes dropped to the papers in my hands, so I started folding them to camouflage them as meaningless trash.

"Yeah."

"Yeah, or yes?"

"Yes, I think so."

"How come you don't know?"

"Because I haven't checked yet."

"So you haven't read your Psalm or Proverbs since Monday morning?"

"No."

"What do you mean, no?" She was baiting me now.

"What are those papers?"

"Financial aid stuff."

"Financial aid stuff for what? Give 'em here!"

"I have to tell you something," I said, already cornered.

"Tell me what? Let me see those papers!"

It was time.

I said it slowly and deliberately—without a stutter or a wobble.

"Mom, please listen. I'm going to live with Daddy so I can go to Cal State Fullerton."

She paused, raising both hands to her hips.

"Go get in the car, now! We're going to bible study."

"What?" My voice climbed. "Mom, didn't you hear what I just said?

I'm not going to any bible study tonight, or ever, and I'm not going to that church anymore, either. I'm going to live with my dad, and I'm going to a real college."

Hissing through clenched teeth, she said, "You can't do *anything* without my permission, boy."

Then, stepping closer, the ghetto broke through. "What the fuck you think this is, nigga?"

I cocked my head, chin up, eyes down on her, and blew a defiant huff.

"You wanna make a bet?"

The snap in my voice was new to both of us. The look in her eyes told me I'd unlocked a level of fury I'd never seen from her before.

But, just like that, I wasn't afraid of her anymore. It was the moment her spell of intimidation was broken.

Fists balled, she lunged for me, moving with determined speed. She seemed to vanish and then materialize again like a vampire, right in front of me, bearing her teeth, ready to sink them into my neck to drain the life out of me. But not before she would get a few good licks in, in sure. Right across my face, or on the top of my head, just for old times' sake.

Maybe she'd finish me by snapping my neck right after punching me in the chest like that time in Jr. High when she cracked one of my ribs in the car for ditching school.

Then, she could go right ahead with pouring out my life's

blood from the severed veins of my bent throat and get it the hell over with.

Why did she get so much satisfaction from thwarting any opportunity for me to explore my potential?

Why was she so determined in this moment to be the villain in the story of my coming of age?

"You not goin' anywhere unless I say so."

I repeated myself, "You wanna make a bet?"

Then, pumph! Right into my chest, she clawed away at the neck of my t-shirt, twisting it into her right hand while holding her left in a tight fist—like a school bully.

I found it quite easy to remove what was now a much smaller, weaker hand than what I had always remembered.

I thought to myself, *Oh damn, I'm pretty strong.*

Dianna was outraged.

She grabbed me by the neck, digging her nails into the skin around my Adam's apple, trying to force my head toward the floor.

That was where she wanted me now—down, cowering at her feet, as if I were the slave and she the master.

Unlucky for her, I wasn't going anywhere.

"Take those papers outta your pocket!" She screamed.

She had another thing coming. I used both hands to shove her off me, planting my palms squarely in the center of her chest.

The force surprised even me. She flew backward and slammed into the closet doors hard enough to knock one of them off its hinges.

Was I the monster now?

I already knew how she would tell this at Word Harvest. She'd glow like a saint in a Titian painting. She'd leave out the choking. She'd say my voice turned demonic. That my eyes went black.

This wasn't a movie. She wasn't a vampire, and neither was I.

But something ugly had been born in that moment—something neither of us had intended or could control.

It fed on my desperation and on Dianna's rage, growing heavier between us with every breath. Fear gave it shape—pressing it into the space we shared, real and undeniable, until the room itself shrank around it.

"I heard you on the phone. You didn't think I knew, huh?"

I laughed. Then I roared in her face.

"I don't *care* if you know!"

"You don't raise your voice to *me* Motherfucker! This is *my* mothafuckin' house boy. You will obey me under my mothafuckin'..."

I cut her right off, "I'm leavin' on Saturday anyway!"

"Shut your fuckin' mouth, you smart assed Faggot, you not goin' nowhere!"

*What a minute, what did she just call me?*

"Fuck you!" I screamed.

Those two words came up the soles of my feet like thunder travelling through my whole body.

She cursed me right back, too. Just like we were two hoes, yelling in the street.

"Fuck you, Faggot! Yeah Faggot!" "You disgusting fucking Faggot!"

There she was. The Dianna that I always knew. The gloves came off completely.

She must have been saving this one up for a while, this bite she would take out of me.

The way she relished in calling me that word, with an ardent grin of satisfaction stretched across her already flushed countenance.

Like the face you make when you smell a clean towel pulled right out of the dryer after it beeps. This felt good to her, but it couldn't hurt me.

Did she forget what happened when I was in the third grade? Well, I didn't.

"Mommy, what is a Faggot?"

"Where did you hear that word from?"

"A boy at school named Seth called me Faggot, Faggot, Faggot until I hit him in the mouth."

"Did you get in trouble?"

"No."

"Good. Go get the dictionary so we can look it up."

"Faggot. A bundle of sticks or twigs bound together and used as fuel."

"There, you see, that's what the word Faggot means."

"That's just stupid to call someone. Why would he call me that?"

"Because he's jealous of you."

Was she the one who was jealous now? Jealous because I was getting the hell out of Pomona—that I was going off to college despite her plan? Maybe she was just jealous that I had enough common sense to know better than she did at my age.

I stood there fearless before her, all lit up, igniting her insidious, narcissistic jealousy into flames. I guess I was the fuel after all.

The Faggot. And proud of it.

# LEAVING, GONE, FREE

"**Y**ou packed up all your shit? Good!"

The fallen closet door exposed the hefty bags I had filled with my things.

I noticed Dion and Brianna standing in the doorway, hands cupped over their ears, so I said nothing.

"You know homosexuals go straight to hell, right?"

Still, I said nothing.

"Well, you can take your faggot ass straight to hell!" She continued.

"You think you're gonna go live out there and do whatever the fuck you want, don't you?"

She was having a conversation with herself, which was making her go absolutely batshit.

"Answer me, boy!"

Nothing she tried was working, so she took it to the next level.

"Go on then, you disgusting faggot," she screamed. "Get the fuck out! Get your nasty, disgusting, demonic ass out of my house."

Then, using what she had learned about the power of the blood of Jesus, she straightened her arm toward me as if to wield a magical spell.

"I bind this homosexual spirit from my home in the name of Jesus, never to return again!"

With that, she started chucking my things out of the closet while speaking in tongues. That's when Dion and Brianna started pleading.

"Mommy, please, Mommy, stop."

Their soft, sorrowful voices couldn't penetrate the energy of hate or the savagery it takes to throw your eldest child out of the house.

The good oldest child who cooks, cleans, babysits, and irons. Your oldest boy, who never bullies his little brother, who combs his baby sister's hair before school.

The son who has been there through the good and the bad, the easy and the rough.

Once she got the bags out of the closet, that wasn't enough.

Ripping into them, she began flinging things one by one, saying, "I bought this, I bought this, I bought this!"

A shoe. A sock. A pair of pants. Some underwear.

Each thing she found, she claimed, like she had a fixation on inanimate objects. Most of those things I had bought with my own money from working as a telemarketer at Olan Mills.

She's the one who told me, "Since you have your own money now, you can pay your own tithes and offerings and buy your own school clothes."

It didn't matter. I was glad she was having a breakdown. And if there was anything I could have done to make it permanent — so she could be put in a loony bin — I would have done it.

"Stop throwing my things everywhere!"

With that, she changed tactics, scooped up an armful, and

headed out of the bedroom. I heard the front door open, then slam against the wall.

Through the bathroom window, I watched the fabric sail through the air and land with a plop on the walkway.

"Get the fuck out!" She hollered, over and over.

Now that she was outside, she could draw an audience, so she got louder.

Reality hit me like a bolt of lightning. I didn't need any of these things. They were just things. She was throwing meaningless shit across the front yard, and showing any connection to it only gave her more power.

Man, she was fucked up.

I yelled out the window, "I was leavin' anyway, bitch!

"Who you callin' a bitch, bitch? I'll show you a bitch!"

I ran outside to meet her. I wanted her to "show" me, so I could "show" her too.

We met at the threshold of the front door. As she pulled me out, I pushed right into her.

We rolled onto the grass like two dogs fighting over a piece of meat. Popping back to our feet, we spread apart.

The neighbor across the street came out and stood watching.

"You wanna disrespect me, you can get the fuck out of my house, punk fuckin' faggot."

"I *am* out!"

As I bent over to pick up my things, that's when I felt her arms wrap around my neck in a chokehold. I tried to bite her, but I couldn't get my chin down far enough, so I dropped my weight backward and slipped free.

"Hey, let him alone," the man across the street yelled.

I could barely breathe, but I managed to scream out to her:

"Okay! You wanna fight me like that? Let's go then, bitch!"

With one giant step forward, I slapped the living shit out of her face. She fell into me instead of away, but it didn't snap her out of it the way I half-hoped it would.

She grabbed my hair and pulled me down into the grass, forcing my face into the mud. I felt the grit scrape my skin, smelled the grass—felt it poke into my eye as I blinked it away.

With the side of her other hand, she punched my head and my back, pounding again and again.

I curled tighter and tighter into a ball, like when I was a little boy, trying to make myself small enough to disappear. Small enough not to feel anything at all.

The neighbors shouted for her to stop.

"Please, ma'am!"

"Stop, or we'll call the police!"

They didn't know Dianna. Did they?

She beat me like an animal. Like a slave trying to escape newly realized freedom. And let's face it — that's all I had ever been to her. A slave. A smiling, useful, smart, funny, mannerly slave.

So, with the greatest abandon I had ever known, I matched her energy.

In a mad fury, I kicked, slapped, and punched in syncopation with my words.

"Get offa me, bitch!"

Boom, boom, boom — the bass line.

"Get offa me, bitch!" — the melody, written in three-four time.

I had her hair wrapped so tightly in my fingers that I could speak directly into her ear.

"I hate you!"

Her wince inspired a repeated chorus.

"I hate you. I hate you. I hate yoooooooouuuuuuuuuu!"

Then I did it — something I had always been living inside me. I finally released what had been festering inside of me for all these years, and I took my revenge.

**Pop. Pop. Pop. Pop. Pop. Pop. Pop. Pop**.

Eight times to the top of her head this time. Then I shoved her away from me, far enough so that she could look me straight in my eyes. That way, she'd remember the satisfied look on my face forever.

I stood over her, repeating, "I hate you," like I was in a trance.

That's when I saw Brian pull up in his white Ford Probe.

"Paul! Get in the car!"

I knew what it meant. I knew what would happen once I did.

I would be free.

But then Dion and Brianna appeared in the doorway.

"Paulie, don't go!"

Dion was choking on his words. Brianna stood frozen, fists pressed to her forehead, crying as if she had just watched me die.

"Is this your stuff?" Brian asked, scooping it up anyway.

Dion ran back inside, and I snapped out of it.

Then he came running again, waving two one-dollar bills.

"Paulie, take this with you."

As I took the money from his hand, Dianna spat in my face and yanked him away.

"Let's go!" Brian said.

I got into the car. Shut the door. Rolled up the window.

Zhane came on the radio.

"Love me today and hate me tomorrow…"

Can you please take me over to the new Jack in the Box?

Yea man. Brian looked like he'd seen fifteen ghosts all at once.

"You alright in there?" Brian tapped on the locked bathroom door.

"I'll be out in a second."

The running water made me have to go pee, but for some reason, I held it until I was done washing my face and hands, knowing that after I finally did take a piss, I'd have to wash them again anyway. I didn't have anything else to do. I couldn't even remember what I was supposed to be doing. I made my way over to the booth where Brian was sitting.

"They're out of strawberry, so I got you vanilla."

"Okay." There was a long, relaxing silence between us, then, as calmly as he could and without sounding nosey, Brian was hoping to make some sense of all this. He asked, "Paul…what happened?"

"I told my mom I wanted to go live with my dad, so we got into a fight."

"What?"

"Yeah. I still have to call him. Do you have any change?"

"Here, go look in the ashtray."

Brian handed me his keys, so I went to sort through his change for a few quarters. Calling my dad felt like being in a dream. I don't know if the adrenaline in my body was wearing off, but I spoke very slowly, without much detail, with a sort of haze all around me.

"Don't leave there, son, I'll be right there."

My dad grew up in Pomona, so he knew where the corner of Towne Avenue and the 10 freeway was. That was enough of a description, so I went back inside and ate every bit of that food Brian had bought for me while I told him exactly everything that happened. This way, Dianna wouldn't be able to get away with the fake story I knew she would tell his mom, Winna.

His eyes got big, and his neck stretched out a little when I said certain things. I told him, slowly moving through it piece by piece, starting with the bullshit the so-called prophet had to say, all the way up until the part when I heard him call my name from his car.

"Damn!" He said in a powerful whisper. "Paul… Dianna did you like that?"

"Yes, Brian. She's *been* doin' me like that. Just this time, I was done."

"You always look so happy, man. I'm sorry, I never knew that."

"It's okay, Brian, nobody knew because I kept it a secret."

And just like that, reality hit. Boys like me who are abused behind closed doors—we don't get happy send-offs.

We get nothing. Not a goddamn thing but maybe an ass-whoopin'.

Part of the cost I paid to be free.

# LOVE, LOVE, LOVE

"Just come live at my house."

"What about James?"

"He's on my damn nerves. I was gonna tell him being roommates wasn't working out anyway."

"Well then, he'll hate me."

"So!"

"What do you mean, *so*? I like James."

"Do you want to stay at Gran's, sleeping on her sofa, or come here, have a room to yourself, and some privacy?"

"You're right." I paused. "I want privacy. I want my life back. I want to start over. I'll move in until I save up enough money to get back to Long Beach. I gotta get back to the ocean."

I met my best friend, Donald, while working at Macy's years earlier. I was eighteen then, newly back in Pomona after a failed attempt at university, a relationship with a swindler named Patrick, and a brief, lonely stint living alone in downtown Long Beach.

By now, I was twenty-four. I'd just left another boyfriend and was starving for friends, attention, and relief. I drank every night without exception. Around that time, Donald was on paid administrative leave from work after a slick preacher accused him of something untrue, temporarily costing him his badge.

So while he didn't have to work—and because misery loves company—we went out nearly every day. Picking up guys. Driving drunk—calling it fun.

The kind of fun people mistake during youth, when really it's desperation dressed up as freedom.

Donald was fifteen years older than me, thirty-nine, and still keeping pace, mostly because I dragged him into the same old bars so men could buy me drinks and take me home to fuck the living daylights out of me.

When I look back at the effort I put into drinking myself to death, I'm struck by how methodical it was. I convinced myself that if I could find the right amount, the right combination, I would pass out one night and simply never wake up.

I imagined leaving this planet cleanly—ascending to nirvana with my young, beautifully dead body left behind, free from the burden of questioning everything about myself.

I would become stardust again.

No more memories of the hand or the hairbrush crashing down on my head. No more hiding in the crack of the coat closet, listening to yelling and glass breaking. No more lying in bed at night, sobbing silently, controlling my breath so I wouldn't scream from the pain.

And then, one day—quiet as the midnight tide—I was sick of my broken alcoholic self.

There was no grand epiphany. No dramatic turning point. I had already cried all the tears many times before.

I decided to change, and then kept deciding, second by second. I used my magic again, only this time for myself. I opened the gate to understanding my worth, and it was shockingly difficult but much easier than drinking, crying, fighting, running, and snorting coke.

Easier than all of the effort I was making at slowly killing myself.

I tried AA. But at first It didn't work for me.

The jaded Queens of the Alano Club Realm told me I was much too happy, too grateful, too put together. My teeth were too white. My body was too intact to be taken as a serious alcoholic. Whatever the fuck that meant.

One old man refused to sponsor me. From behind his black coffee and cigarette, he said, "Let me know when you wake up in a dumpster with your asshole on fire, honey, then we'll talk."

Hard pass.

So I ditched AA and went on a binge in Arizona with a handsome culinary-school classmate named Christopher—sexy, stylish, straight, just how I liked them.

We had a blast until the cocaine, Courvoisier, and chaos turned me whiny and needy.

I left for Palm Springs.

There, I lived in a sober men's group home for six months, watching the other guys fall off the wagon left and right—they complained about pool duty, house rules, and snuck into the bathrooms giving blowjobs in exchange for Xanax.

What saved me were the classes at Michael's House Rehabilitation Center. Donald pulled strings through his L.A. County Sheriff connections; otherwise, I never could have afforded it.

They taught me that *the middle* was a safe place to live. For the first time, someone addressed the root of my drinking instead of merely slapping a label on it.

At off-site meetings, people complained so much when they shared that I sang songs in my head while they were talking. I volunteered to bring cupcakes so I could stay busy and focused.

Everything was chalked up to the disease. No responsibility. No excavation. That didn't sit right with me.

Growth takes work. Real work.

You can't stay sober if you're a punk.

I started doing mirror affirmations. Then writing them down in what I called my *Drunk Journals*. I got better at listening. Letting others shine. Living without armor. I craved the serenity of it all.

One afternoon, eating my sukiyaki in silence, a guy from the house came up to me.

"Hey, girl."

"Terri, don't call me girl."

"Okay then, *man*."

Terri—rugged, street-smart, manipulative, wounded. I had a soft spot for him, but I kept my distance.

"Have you heard of the Palm Canyon Theatre?"

He told me they were auditioning for *Miss Saigon*.

I laughed. "I hate musicals."

"Then just come with me." I can't read music, and I don't know anybody there."

An hour later, I wound up being convinced to belt *America the Beautiful* in the director's office.

Just like that, I became a musical theatre guy.

Eventually, I returned to Long Beach. Sober. Selling home-made cookies. Starting over, I joined the Orange County Gay Men's Chorus: Men Alive.

I had no idea my life was about to change.

It was mid-September. The Santa Anas were blowing. I arrived early, sneaking a cigarette near the side of the building when I saw him—tall, blond, quiet, holding the door for others.

Time slowed.

Light gathered around him.

"Oh my fucking God," I whispered to myself. "That's the man I'm going to marry."

I followed him inside, watched him settle into the Bass section, nodding politely, smiling softly. I put my knees on the chair in front of him.

"Hi. I'm Paul."

His face lit up into the most beautiful, boyish smile I had ever seen.

Nice to meet you, I'm George.

We carpooled. We spent nights together. Everything was easy. Too easy.

No yelling. No grabbing. No drama. He respected my boundaries. He listened. He let me change my mind.

So, naturally, I broke up with him.

"He has to be a serial killer," I told Donald.

Donald stared at me. "Paulie, I never thought I would say this to you, but you're being stupid."

He was right.

I called George.

We've been together ever since.

Sometimes it takes a friend who knows your whole story to help you win.

Donald helped me win the greatest prize of my life—a man filled with love.

# UNC BONES CRIB

 ears into my sobriety, I decided it was time to see my family again. I traveled alone, crossing the country from Florida back to Pomona for the family reunion.

That morning was overcast. I woke early so I could stop at Samo's while the fryer oil was still fresh and order the onion rings my daddy and I used to love so much.

Standing on the corner of Garey and Franklin, greasy bag in hand, I devoured those golden rings whose smell and taste I had never forgotten. When the bag was empty, I decided I would finally go face-to-face with my old neighborhood.

The Angelos and I needed to come to an understanding, once and for all.

The place that could have swallowed me whole needed to see me arrive intact. It needed to smell my cologne, notice my coordinated outfit, and register the confident swagger of a proud, put-together gay man.

It needed to acknowledge me as one of the few surviving sons of its streets.

So there I was, forty-something years later. As I turned onto

Angela Street, the fear and pride dissolved, and I was suddenly a little boy again.

The neighborhood looked worse than it had when I was a child. I understood why, but understanding didn't soften it.

Most of the buildings were still the same dull color, never repainted. Cracks exposed stucco and rusted rebar at the corners. Where grass or ivy once grew, there were now pavers or bare dirt.

We hadn't had much back then—it was the ghetto—but we kept it neat. When I reached my childhood home, it looked impossibly small. I felt foolish for letting this place and what happened here haunt me for so long.

I parked my rental car across the street and gave myself a pep talk in the mirror. I wasn't there to cry. I was a grown-ass man now. I was strong. I had escaped this place. I reminded myself of what I'd accomplished.

By nineteen, I was making more money than my parents combined at a Fortune 500 company. I served in the U.S. Navy during Don't Ask, Don't Tell and thrived. I graduated at the top of my culinary class and became an executive chef before even finishing school.

When I wanted another craft, I mastered floristry and ran the wedding and special events department of a nationwide company in Tampa.

My husband and I own our home. I'm even the president of our HOA.

*"Now get out of this goddamn car, Paul."*

I caught sight of the apartment walkway from the rear-view mirror—the place where I once skipped, ran, and played freeze-tag.

*"Open the door... Get out. Get out!"*

That was when I remembered why I was there in the first place: to face the secret thing that happened to me one night, fast yet lasting forever. The only thing I didn't speak about to anyone else, my whole life.

Years ago, Dianna took a job at Susie's Casuals, the newest women's store at Indian Hill Mall. Young, fashionable, and pretty, she landed the job easily.

Though it meant working nights, she must have believed Daddy could handle a little responsibility. Don't ask what inspired that faith, other than desperation. We needed money, and since my father wouldn't get a second job, she did.

"There's tuna casserole in the oven," she said. "Just put it on a plate."

"Yeah, okay, Mommy," Big Paul replied with a smile.

"Be good for your dad. Brianna's at Valentina's. I love you."

"Love you," Dion and I said together.

As we ate, our father transformed into Pena—the mischievous version of himself we loved and resented. He drifted from window to window, corner to corner, restless.

The TV and radio were both off, unusual for dinnertime.

"Mommy usually puts the stereo on." I reminded him.

"You wanna come with me?" he asked, playfully.

We were thrilled.

Living with him didn't mean spending time with him, especially at night. Still, I worried about where he might take us.

The last time he went out alone with me was to a girlfriend's house, where he planted me in front of the TV with a Capri Sun and Junior Mints while they bumped uglies behind her bedroom door.

I didn't want trouble with my little brother there. "Where are we going?"

"Unc Bones crib."

"Unc Bones, Daddy?"

My voice tightened, my speech slightly slurred by a loose front tooth.

"Isn't that where they do drugs?" I rolled the tooth with my tongue.

He knew I knew he was one of them.

He laughed. "Nah, Wally Gator. Just a few beers."

A lie. A few beers meant a case. Then weed. Then cocaine. I knew it, but eight-year-olds weren't supposed to say that.

"What's wrong with your mouth?"

"My tooth's loose."

"Lemme see." He laughed like an older brother, tugging my lip down. "Yeah. It's loose."

"Can I bring my crayons?"

"Yeah."

The California sunset was slipping away behind the neighborhood, somewhere near where the 60 and 71 freeways meet. Night crept in, and men shed their daytime faces. Smiles flattened. Voices changed. They leaned against poles and garage doors, relieved by the cover of darkness.

By night, the Daddies, uncles, and cousins filled their lungs with weed smoke and burned chemicalized cocaine from glass pipes, daring each other to cough—or not to. Who could last the longest? Who didn't care who heard?

Under the slick purple-black sky, these men became like warlocks, though each was somebody's someone by day, the night darkened them. To their lonely women watching commercials and pretending not to care, they became "that nigga drinkin' in the alley" or Red the dope man instead of our neighbor, Randy's dad.

Streetlights hummed with an amber glow, transforming the bigger kids into lil' murderers, as they now called themselves. Teenagers drunk on that Olde E jacked cars, twisted fingers into signs, and claimed colors, changing mere red and blue into death and war. Especially blue.

Bullets don't know boundaries nor allegiance, so we dove into clean white bathtubs that smelled of Comet, cold as empty unlined caskets—with all of it happening on any given ordinary Tuesday.

"Come on, Jing-Jing. Let's go, Paulie."

At home I was Paulie. Outside, I was Lil' Paul. Neither name hid my skipping, finger-popping, or random twirling outbursts very well.

I stuffed my backpack with crayons, coloring books, and He-Man figures. We passed our old apartment—dark, hollow, unfamiliar.

As the concrete walkway turned to asphalt, sloping into a piss-smelling alley, men followed Pena automatically. We picked up friends from doorways and from under streetlights. They slapped hands, bragged, switched to street names.

Whodini was right—the freaks really do come out at night.

Pena didn't mind having us with him either. Not at all. He could bend like a tree if it meant getting drugs and alcohol worked into the equation.

We arrived quickly as Unc Bone's was less than fifty yards away. As we climbed the stairs, the unease bloomed in my stomach. My instincts were screaming at me from the inside.

I reached for Dion's hand, but he pulled away, wanting Daddy's instead. I understood that feeling.

The smell lingering in the air thickened—chemical, heavy. Even now, it clings to memory. Music played softly inside, highlighted by voices louder than the stereo. The door opened without us knocking, and just like that, we were swallowed up by the dank, dreary world of a crack house called Unc Bones Crib.

# HIDING DION

"That's Paulie right there. Umm, Humm. That's my baby, and y'all cain't touch him!"

Relieved to see a familiar face, I called out, "Hi Yahzmin!"

"Ooooh, you got your lil' baby brother wichew' too huh?" She was singing her words again.

"Say hi, Dion."

"Hi." Poor Dion's face looked like he was in the middle of a nightmare, and well, he was.

"I used to have a baby brother…" Yahzmin started a story.

"Girl, git yo crazy ass out the way!" One of the men inside ripped into her for standing in the doorway, so I made sure he saw it when I rolled my eyes at him.

"What it is, Lil' Main?" The handsome real-life version of Count Chocula stood in front of me, wearing a tight, tan, V-neck sweater with long sleeves bunched up to the middle of his forearms and a pair of brown slacks creased up to the belt loops.

He was much taller than my daddy, and I think he was a little bit older too, with light skin and "good hair" patted down neatly, just like mine.

A gold stud in his left ear, a thick gold bracelet on his wrist, and a gold pinky ring on his right hand. I figured he knew my dad since everyone always did.

"Y'all want some potato chips?" Dion and I looked at each other and smiled.

"Yes, please," I spoke for both of us as usual. They were Funyun's, like the kind my dad always got too.

This handsome man just handed me his whole newly opened bag of chips and walked away, disappearing along with my father and a couple of other men into one of the bedrooms.

*Maybe he likes me.* I thought.

Yasmin was sitting in the corner, her head turning from side to side to the beat of the music while safely out of the way of everyone else.

I looked around to assess the room. The noise volume was what you could call house party soft, but weeknight loud.

Then the record player stopped, and Yasmin got yelled at again by that same asshole in the living room.

"Go change the album!" He glared at her and sucked his teeth. So, when he walked by me again, I rolled my eyes at him extra hard this time.

I knew I could get away with it, too, because no one messed around with my crazy ass daddy, so this chump wouldn't dare say anything to me.

So that we could stay safe away from the grown-ups, I opened up the coat closet next to the front door so I could make some room for Dion and me.

As many times as I'd seen these little shindigs turn into an all-out brawl, I knew better. One minute, everyone is laughing together, the next, you've got two grown, drunk-ass men squabbling on the floor like two fish out of water.

"Your Daddy wants you."

The handsome man came to get me.

I thought,

*That must mean that he likes me, or something. I mean, he did give me a whole brand-new bag of Funyun's, and he came back to get me just so he could talk to me again.*

As I got up from the floor to walk past him, I got a little pat on my butt. *Yeah, he likes me.*

My dad came busting out the door of the dimly lit bedroom, followed by enough smoke to gag a maggot. He was holding a can of Schlitz Malt Liquor Bull in one hand and smoking the end of a joint with the other.

"Lemme see your tooth, son."

His familiar glassy-eyed grin and slurred speech were taking over

"No, Daddy. You're already drunk."

"Come on, man, I'm not drunk."

He put his arms out for me to come closer and said sweetly, "I'm your dad."

*Yeah, he's drunk.*

"Come here. Let's pull it your tooth out so the tooth fairy can bring you some money, son."

One of the other drunkies called out from the room. "Yeah, tie it up and slam it in the door."

Everybody got involved like they were getting ready to fix a car or paint a house.

"Get some string!"

"What string? Thread?"

"No yarn!"

"Man, ain't nobody got no damn yarn!"

"Where the fuck you think we at, nigga?"

They laughed at one another's suggestions as if they were changing in a locker room. All this while passing a rolled-up dollar bill around, taking turns snorting up the powdery lines skillfully razored from the giant white mound on the mirrored tabletop.

The curtains were drawn, and from the stillness mixed with the B.O. in the room, I could tell that the window was closed too. The closet doors were off the track and nowhere to be found.

Not a stitch of clothing was hanging on the rod either. The shelf above was stacked with lidless shoe boxes, duffel bags, and a weird-looking vase. which was probably a bong.

From his clunky, silver and grey wheelchair in the corner of the room, sitting next to the floor lamp, Unc Bone rasped to life in a phlegmy, worn-out voice to stutter up some words.

"Git some floss."

Mostly bones and sinew, an outline of a man more ghost than flesh. Though he didn't scare me, I never wanted to get close enough to know what he smelled like, either.

Wearing the dirtiest white t-shirt ever, he started coughing up a lung.

A burning Pall Mall dangled from his lips—bouncing as he coughed up a hollow wind, causing ashes to land on the plate of old barbecue in his lap.

The light from above outlined his gaunt face, enhancing the dullness of his salt-and-pepper hair. His natural was nappy and dusty as a runaway slave, in desperate need of some Sta-Sof-Fro and a metal natural comb. Metal, not plastic. Facial hair speckled about his cheeks like bits of hamburger meat scattered on a plate.

His pencil-thin neck looked as though it might snap from the weight of his head—a big, tired-looking dome he could barely balance from all that Hennessey he was drinking. His frail torso was weak.

If you were to lift his shirt, the shoulders on him would be just a horizontal ruler held up by a yardstick.

"Where is it?" My dad asked.

Unc Bone taunted, "Look in the bathroom nigga, damn!"

Now, I was no expert, but it just felt like maybe my tooth wasn't loose enough yet. Like maybe it needed a little while longer with me moving it around with my tongue or gently using my finger to wabble it back and forth side to side, maybe another day or so.

Then, maybe it would be fine to pull, but not yet, but the peanut gallery started chiming in again:

"Make a knot first, then tie it round."

"Here, tie it to the doorknob and slam it real quick."

"He won't feel it."

"That's how my daddy used to do mine."

"Wait a minute!" I said.

"Shouldn't I be on that side of the door?"

"One, Two, Three!" He swung the door away from me as I watched my bloody red tooth fly into the air, bounce off the wall, and land right against the pile of coke on the table.

They all cheered as I smacked my hand over my mouth in outrage.

"Daddy, get my tooth outta that!"

"I got it, I got it, man. Here, go rinse it off. And don't let it go down the drain or the tooth fairy can't come."

There was no step stool in the bathroom, so I carefully placed the tooth next to the sink, then hoisted myself onto the counter to reach the faucet.

I spat the blood out, then I angled my head under the faucet to rinse my mouth. It seemed to take forever for it to stop. "You alright, son?"

I answered with my mouth under the water, "Esss!"

"You got it, son?"

"Esss!"

With the blood stopped, I hopped back down, then pushed the tooth deep into my pocket.

Something was wrong.

I couldn't hear Dion playing with the He-Men we brought. I knew he'd likely be doing that instead of coloring, so I took off down the hall.

When I got out into the dining area, there was the handsome Funyun man, sitting there holding my baby brother on his lap with his grown-up man face way too close to my little brother's baby face, and his baby face didn't look happy about that at all.

Yasmin sat way over on the other side of the living room, looking over at us, rocking back and forth, saying nothing, which said everything to me.

I put on the face I saw my mother use whenever she was mothering:

"Here, give him to me."

Scooping one of my most precious belongings off this stranger's lap, I stood Dion up on his feet, then guided him back into the closet.

"Come here wit' me, y'all," Yahzmin called over to me.

"Girl, if you don't shut up and sit yo' retarded ass back down!"

His words were all too familiar.

"Come here, Lil' Paul. Come wit' me."

In one motion, the tall man rose from his chair, flashed his gleaming white smile directly into my eyes, then signaled with his hand for me to follow him down the hall.

I knew it was either going to be my brother or me. Of course, to save Dion from whatever might happen, I'd have to hide him.

It would have to be me.

"Stay in here and play while I get us some more toys."

Yasmin started Uncle Jams Freak of the Week on the record player as I closed the closet door until I heard the latch click.

The music started: "Got to be, gotta be the freak a, da week, Oooo!

My mother told a story about this song as if I didn't remember it myself, but I didn't mind.

I thought that's what moms were supposed to do when they wanted to dote over you to their friends.

"He was still in diapers. I had Parliament on the stereo, you know, I was cleaning the house. The next thing I knew, I looked… (she'd pause there, acting it all out as she told it) There was Paulie with one of his socks on his little foot and the other one in his hand, dustin' the coffee table with it, and gittin' down, too."

As a little boy, I didn't know that she didn't know I could remember this, too. She never knew that I knew—I had never told her exactly how far back my memories reached. I just thought that because she was my mom, the person that I came from, that she already knew what I carried inside me.

What I didn't know, until it happened, was that this new thing, the thing that was happening right now, was going to forever change this song for me.

# MY BROTHER'S KEEPER

Behind the music, the sounds of schoolboy laughter clattered from the other room, where my dad and his homeboys had lulled themselves into the steady rise and fall of cocaine-inflated storytelling.

Stories bounced around the dope-laden coffee table, passed from one mouth to the next. Long, low *Daaaang's* filled the gaps, followed by high, questioning *No shit?* Laughter crashed over everything, loud enough to drown out normal thought.

All except the man leading me into the empty room with the curtains open and the lights off.

He was bigger than my daddy. A grown man who seemed to like me.

He bent close and whispered neatly in my ear, like we were sharing something exciting.

"Go sit down."

I backed my legs into the Lazy-Boy and eased myself into the corner of it.

I thought he might close the door, but he didn't.

I didn't know what was supposed to happen next. I knew I was curious. I also knew I was afraid of getting in trouble, too.

He smiled at me, the kind of smile you give someone when you're both supposed to be having fun. Then he made me do something I didn't know how to do. When I got it wrong, his hand pressed down on my head.

I reared back. If he messed up my hair, people would know. I patted my little afro back into place, the way I thought it should look.

I didn't quite understand how to do what he wanted, and that made him frustrated, which scared me.

He scooped me up like I weighed nothing, one arm wrapped tight around my torso, pressing his forehead against mine. His mouth was everywhere, wet and heavy, tasting like beer and weed. He licked my face, my nose. Nothing was off limits to him.

My body jerked as he tugged urgently at my pants. I dangled there, fearful, without any control over what may happen next.

He dropped into the armchair and pulled me onto his lap, my legs wrapped around his waist.

There was the sound of him spitting. Then something irreversible happened.

I couldn't even holler.

So I let myself leave.

In my mind, I was somewhere else entirely, dressed in my blue Easter suit, climbing a beautiful staircase that didn't belong to that house. I climbed and climbed until I wasn't inside my body anymore.

From high above, now floating outside of that open window, I could still see the room through the open curtains, billowing slightly in the wind. I looked down at the other me, the one I had left behind.

I hoped he would jab his fingers into that man's eyes and run to get his daddy. But if he couldn't, I understood that too. Maybe he could turn into a statue so he wouldn't feel anything at all.

I told myself it was my fault—that I must have done something wrong. That if I hadn't been so eager, none of this would have happened.

Our thoughts tangled together, me and that little boy I had to leave back in that chair.

*So now what's going to happen?*

*This must be what happens to missing kids.*

*They disappear.*

*Dion's going to tell me "see you when the sun rises" tonight.*

*I'll say it back so he won't know I'm dying.*

*Get up.*

*Get off him.*

*You can do it.*

*Scream...*

"Here. Get up."

The sound of his belt buckle clinked as he closed his fly.

One of my legs was out of my pants. One shoe was gone.

Reality came back slowly, thick and foggy. I couldn't remember if I'd been wearing a belt. I couldn't remember if we had finished dinner. For some reason, I needed to know what time it was.

I tried to fix my clothes, but I wasn't sure if I was actually moving or just thinking about it.

The pain arrived next.

I stood there, frozen, like a character in a video game waiting for the start button. Like if the game began, I'd already be on my last life. Maybe if I didn't move at all, I could stay a little longer. Long enough to see my baby brother again.

He grabbed me by the waist and held me out in front of him, as far away as possible, the way people hold a baby with a dirty diaper.

"Hurry up now."

He rushed me into the bathroom and whispered, "Sit on the toilet for a while. Clean yourself up real good."

I lifted the lid without a sound and sat down like he told me to.

Then his smile vanished. What stood in front of me was something else entirely.

"Sit yo mothafuckin ass right there and shut the fuck up till I leave, boy."

A cold paralysis swept through me.

It was him.

The same kind of words Yahzmin hollered up and down the streets of the Angelos—some of them were mine now, too.

I rested my elbows on my knees, fists under my chin, tapping my feet. One shoe on. One shoe off.

Framed by the dark doorway, he looked both unreal and too real at the same time. Like one of the demonic images in the glossy pages of our old Catholic Bible. The whites of his eyes shone brighter than the grin he flashed before gently closing the door.

He was gone, and I was alone.

I had already accepted that I was going to die. I talked myself through it practically. Still, seeing the blood made my chest tighten. It wasn't a lot, but to a kid, any blood is panic.

I dipped toilet paper into the bowl and wiped quietly. I didn't turn on the sink because there was no lock, and I didn't want anyone walking in, thinking I was only washing my hands.

I wiped until the paper came away clean, folded what was left into my underwear to catch anything else, then carefully pulled my pants up.

The pain dulled when I stood, but it came back when I bent to grab my shoe.

That's when I remembered…

"My tooth!" I yelled out while jamming my hand into my pocket.

It was still there.

Making a big deal out of something small gave me a moment of relief. Pretending nothing else had happened helped me reach the next second. Then the next.

I was alive. The bleeding had stopped.

I tucked the tooth away—a tiny piece of me from before.

Dion was still there too, right where I'd left him. Intact.

The men began spilling out of the other room. Pena might have been more than drunk, but he knew better than to have us home late.

I repacked my backpack with the toys and crayons. I straightened Dion's clothes and smoothed his fro while he rubbed his eyes, ready for bed.

I had made the right choice in protecting my baby brother.

Holding my daddy's hand, guiding his drunk, high self toward home, we stepped outside.

Yahzmin stood in the doorway smoking, staring into the star-speckled sky, talking softly.

At first, I wasn't sure if she was talking to a real person or one of the many who inhabited her mind. Then I made out what she was saying.

"It's alright, baby,"

She sang it, almost like a negro spiritual.

"It's gon' be alright now."

"Yahzmin know."

"Wooo, chile'. Yahzmin know."

Yeah, she was talking to a real person all along. She was talking to me.

# IN SAECULA SAECULORUM

Forcing myself out of the car, I accidentally slammed the car door too hard behind me.

There it was: 2385 Chanslor Street, the place where I was brought home from the hospital as an infant.

I took in a deep breath as nostalgia washed over me, heavy and disorienting, like what I imagined a black hole might feel like in outer space. The morning air was fragrant with the same jacaranda trees I once climbed, their scent reminding my fingers what it felt like to squish the fallen purple blooms beneath them.

Those same tree trunks still offered outstretched limbs, dappled in textured leaves—trembling lightly in the breeze. Overnight dew left the soil wet in the same way it always had, giving off the familiar smell of clean dirt and dryer lint, as we used to say. The front lawn looked so small, it made me laugh out loud.

I was doing just fine until I looked beneath the kitchen window and saw that the old, raised brick flower bed was gone. My grandmother's rose bushes were gone. I bit my lip.

Her recent passing helped push me here, in search of closure.

After caring for her during the last six months of her life, she died reluctantly, yet comfortably, in my arms as I sang her a Gladys Knight song.

I had planned to knock on the door and offer money for those bushes, then figure out a way to ship them home. But like her, they were gone now. It was more than I could take. I sat down on the walkway step the way I used to, though now my knees were much closer to my face. I gathered myself.

Old ghosts called me on a slow walk down the concrete path alongside the complex. I ran my palm over the place where the mailboxes used to be and stood where a cactus bed once lived—now paved over. I traced the old fence my father and grandfather had built, pretending I was touching their hands through all the time, space, and worlds now between us. I sat on the gravel steps where I used to do my homework.

Closing my eyes, I remembered the loquat tree Aunt Gina planted, and how in that moment I missed her. I missed Yahzmin coming to sit beside me, too. All of it was gone now. Even the ivy had been torn out and replaced with thick-bladed grass, now neglected and overgrown.

Instead of cutting through the alley, I took the long way around the corner toward Unc Bone's. The boys who once lived there had long since met their fates, either in prison or by death.

I was the only survivor.

Along the block, the other rose bushes were still there, blooming as they always had. I passed the twin olive tree where Reggie once got his foot stuck and looked for the metal utility cover we'd wedged into its bark. It was still there. The tree had grown calmly around it, holding it in place because no one had ever returned it to where it belonged.

I walked on with a new resolve—to face my demons, to lay this trauma back down where it had been shackled to me.

No longer would I drag through life this rape, this violation, this invisible monster that whispered behind me in the mirror, drunk or sober, day and night, telling me I was damaged goods, that I deserved my suffering.

To stand up for that little boy—and for all the little boys—I decided I would speak to this place.

*You have no power over me. I release you.*

I would say it aloud, even if a million eyes were watching. But the streets were empty that overcast morning in The Angelo's. Not one human soul was out.

It was as if the neighborhood itself had stepped aside, granting me the space I needed to heal. A blank canvas for a new memory, gilded in gold—the color of enlightenment, the color my heart needed to mend.

When I reached the place where it had all happened, I finally lifted my eyes.

I stopped short.

Tears filled my vision as my pace quickened to a trot, then slowed again. I stepped through someone else's yellow wildflowers and nasturtiums as though I had planted them myself. An unfamiliar wrought-iron gate stood before me, but I barely noticed it.

I wrapped both hands around the spiked bars.

It was gone.

Demolished.

Once, it had traveled the world with me, woven into the fibers of my haunted soul. It had justified my suicidal alcoholism, hollowed at the bottom of every glass. It hovered in bathwater the night I almost slipped away. It stared back at me in the faces of men I let use my body.

I held on so I wouldn't collapse from the shock.

For a brief moment, sunlight broke through the gray clouds and spilled across the ground. I stepped into it.

The vindication was indescribable.

In that moment, I understood the memory no longer had power over me. My scars could become symbols of survival—proof that broken-hearted people still shine, still mend, still rise.

It was the only apartment complex in The Angelo's that had been erased entirely.

In its place stood a miracle of irony and grace: Esperanza y Alegría Park.

Hope and Happiness.

I laughed, almost expecting to wake up. There was a half basketball court, a small play area, two neon-yellow slides, and a climbing wall.

I spent an entire lifetime wishing that I could change what happened to me. Making up better stories to hear with prettier words to tell the shiny new, unblemished people I met along the way in exchange for their smiles filled with embrace.

Only now, all I want to do is reclaim that time—using it instead to revel in my strength, the glory of my resilience under the pressure I was formed in.

This spark—fanned by sober living, ruthless self-honesty, and a stubborn commitment to love over fear—has grown into a steady flame. The remnants of my past are what forged me into the man I am today, and for myself, I am grateful.

So this is what we survivors should hear—the sons and brothers, the cousins and uncles, the fathers and friends—and to the women who love them:

You are not the sum of what happened to you. There is more. You are more.

You are whole.

You are intact.

You are loved, and you *can* still love.

On that same trip to Pomona, I learned that 1388 Murchinson Avenue—where my mother was raped and beaten—and Word

Harvest Worship Church, the place that divided us and taught me hate instead of love, had also been erased.

Murchinson was now a leveled field. The church lay in graffiti-covered rubble, rebar jutting like exposed bone from a ransacked grave.

I was stunned. Giddy even. Convinced I had conjured it with the same stubborn magic that saved me throughout life and all the way up to that very moment.

The hope I drowned in each glass of Courvoisier.

The tears I had cried by the bucketful.

The molten truth I poured over my wounds—and survived.

Now, I lovingly recall the old wounds that fought time to stay with me. The battle scars of my youth that cut me so deeply.

I wear them proudly.

They are my golden bruises.


**THE END**

www.ingramcontent.com/pod-product-compliance
Lightning Source LLC
Chambersburg PA
CBHW031019160726
47991CB00005B/1787